LIFE AFTER DEATH

tony cooke

life after death

REDISCOVERING LIFE AFTER THE LOSS OF A LOVED ONE

With a New Format

FAITH LIBRARY PUBLICATIONS®

18   17   16   15   14   13   12   12   11   10   09   08   07   06

Life After Death
ISBN-13: 978-0-89276-966-7
ISBN-10: 0-89276-966-1

Copyright © 2003 Rhema Bible Church
AKA Kenneth Hagin Ministries, Inc.
All rights reserved.
Printed in USA

In the U.S. write:
Kenneth Hagin Ministries
P.O. Box 50126
Tulsa, OK 74150-0126
1-888-28-FAITH
www.rhema.org

In Canada write:
Kenneth Hagin Ministries of Canada
P.O. Box 335, Station D
Etobicoke (Toronto), Ontario
Canada M9A 4X3
1-866-70-RHEMA
www.rhemacanada.org

DEDICATION

To my parents, Kenneth and Barbara Cooke . . . Thank you for your love and support and for the values you instilled in my life.

Blessed be the God and Father of our Lord Jesus Christ,
the Father of mercies and God of all comfort,
who comforts us in all our tribulation,
that we may be able to comfort those
who are in any trouble, with the comfort
with which we ourselves are comforted by God.

—2 Corinthians 1:3–4

CONTENTS

INTRODUCTION

You may have picked up this book for one of several reasons. Perhaps someone you love has died, and you need comfort in this challenging time, wisdom on how to put matters into perspective, and strength to move on with your life. Maybe you are trying to make sense of what happened, and you wonder if anything will ever be normal again.

Perhaps you have a friend who has lost a loved one and you feel inadequate to help him or her. Your heart goes out to your friend, but you just don't know what to say. It is also possible that you simply desire to be better prepared and equipped for helping others when the inevitable losses of life occur.

This book will not answer every conceivable question, and it is not a magic wand that will instantly make the pain vanish. Neither will it provide you with a quick fix for a friend who is hurting. But in this book you will find insights from God's Word and reflections from those who have walked the road you are now walking. I believe these insights will be a source of strength, comfort, and valuable information to you in your journey.

In more than twenty-five years of ministry, I have been with many families before, during, and after the death of their loved ones. I have witnessed both the human pain of loss and the divine comfort offered by the Holy Spirit. Gratefully, I was also able to include the wisdom that others have gained through their experience with loss. Many people offered their personal stories and insights, which are shared freely throughout this book. I greatly appreciate their openness and willingness to share from their experiences so that we may all benefit.

There are many different types of loss in life that affect us. Some people are laid off from jobs, others experience divorce, some have prized possessions stolen, and others have a home destroyed by fire or natural disaster. While this book emphasizes issues pertaining to the death of a loved one, it should be noted that any type of loss could trigger reactions in our lives.

Though each of us experiences different types of loss in life, the comfort and strength of God are available to us all. As you read through these pages, my prayer is that you will allow God to speak to you through His Word and by His Spirit. He alone fully comprehends the intricacies of your individual personality and the specific nature of what you are experiencing.

God understands where you are right now in your particular situation. He doesn't expect any one person to experience grief recovery in the exact same way someone else did. He loves you for who you are, and He understands the times and seasons of your life—as well as each factor that makes you a unique individual.

May the Father of mercies and God of all comfort minister to you through this book. May He strengthen you and enable you to comfort others with the same comfort by which He has comforted you (2 Corinthians 1:3–4).

Part 1

MATTERS OF THE SOUL

chapter 1

THIS CAN'T BE HAPPENING!
(DEALING WITH SHOCK)

Hear my cry, O God; Attend to my prayer.
From the end of the earth I will cry to You,
When my heart is overwhelmed;
Lead me to the rock that is higher than I.
For You have been a shelter for me,
A strong tower from the enemy.
I will abide in Your tabernacle forever;
I will trust in the shelter of Your wings.

—Psalm 61:1–4

In the Book of Psalms, David described times when his heart was overwhelmed. Many translations of the Bible use the term "faint" or "heart-fainting" to refer to this overwhelming feeling. Upon receiving traumatic or distressing news, our mind and body can adversely react in diverse ways. People have described their feelings of shock in various terms. Some say they are stunned; others say disbelief. And some say life seems unreal.

5

"I'll wake up and find out that none of this really happened; it was just a bad dream. It's like I'm not even here and this really isn't happening."

"I'm totally numb. I'm going through the motions, but none of it makes sense. I feel like a robot. I can't think clearly, and I can't seem to make decisions or concentrate. My mind seems fuzzy."

These types of statements are frequently expressed when people receive life-impacting news, like that involving the death of a loved one. The sense of shock and disbelief is especially strong when there is no advance warning of the loss and the news is totally unexpected. One person said the following:

"The suddenness of the death of my grandmother made it very difficult to accept her death. I had no preparation for the abruptness or the nature of her death (she was killed by a drunk driver), and the shock that followed was especially strong."

While grieving the loss of loved ones is a common experience, keep in mind that everyone's experience is different. Others have described their time following the death of their loved ones in the following ways.

"The sense of being totally stunned was unbelievable . . . . It was like I'd gotten the wind knocked out of me."

"At a time when I could barely think or feel any emotion, everyone kept asking me if I was all right, and if I needed anything. I was in so much shock that I didn't know what I needed. I just wanted to withdraw myself."

"Someone told me, 'It's okay to cry,' and I thought, 'Cry? Why haven't I cried?' and I began to feel guilty. Now I realize I was only numb. It took some time before I really let go and cried. Also, I remember initially feeling like I didn't know

what to feel. I wanted to laugh, cry, and scream all at the same time. It was so confusing, but God helped me through."

One author described this sense of numbness and disbelief as an "anesthetic" and as a "psychological shock absorber" that creates "an insulation from the reality of the death until one is more able to tolerate what one doesn't want to believe."[1] In describing just how overwhelmed a person can be at this time another author said, *"The mind is so busy grappling with the ugliness of death, attempting to accept it, and coming to terms with it, that there can be little physical energy left. Grievers are often disorganized, disoriented, and unable to plan even the smallest of tasks."*[2]

Since shock is a common experience in dealing with loss, we can be comforted in knowing that we are not abnormal if we encounter some of these feelings.

SHOCK OR GRACE?

Over the years, I've heard many people testify that God's presence and grace were especially strong toward them in the first few days following the death of a loved one. They were actually surprised at how well they did in the days following the death of their loved one. It was as though God was giving them a special measure of grace for an especially challenging time in life. Though strong emotions may have come later, some of these individuals mentioned not feeling intense emotions early on.

Some might argue that such people are merely in a state of shock and that reality simply hasn't "hit them yet." I don't think it's important to debate whether the person is "just in shock" or if they are genuinely experiencing God's comforting and shielding presence in a unique way. However, it seems completely consistent with God's nature for Him to supernaturally

7

comfort His children and allow them to experience His peace, which surpasses all understanding" (Philippians 4:7).

In Psalm 46, the psalmist describes a very tumultuous and turbulent situation, but his awareness of God's supernatural presence and comfort is also very apparent in the passage.

PSALM 46:1–5,10–11

1 God is our refuge and strength, A very present help in trouble.

2 Therefore we will not fear, Even though the earth be removed, And though the mountains be carried into the midst of the sea;

3 Though its waters roar and be troubled, Though the mountains shake with its swelling.

4 There is a river whose streams shall make glad the city of God, The holy place of the tabernacle of the Most High.

5 God is in the midst of her, she shall not be moved; God shall help her, just at the break of dawn. . . .

10 Be still, and know that I am God; I will be exalted among the nations, I will be exalted in the earth!

11 The Lord of hosts is with us; The God of Jacob is our refuge.

Even in the most traumatic of situations, God is with us. He is our refuge and an ever-present help in trouble. Whether or not we *feel* His presence, we can be confident that He will never leave us or forsake us (Hebrews 13:5).

GOD'S GRACE IS CONSISTENT

The adult son of a friend of mine was killed in a plane crash. When my friend received word of the tragedy, he immediately went to the state where his son had lived and helped his daughter-in-law with the funeral arrangements.

He stayed for a couple of weeks and did all he could to minister to her and assist with the transitions and adjustments his daughter-in-law and his grandchildren would be making.

He commented that while he was there, he sensed an enormous amount of strength and peace. A few days after he returned to his home, he noticed a "let-down" reaction as all of the emotions began to affect him. He said the contrast was so sharp that it almost felt like God's presence had left him. However, he knew the Bible and knew that God was still with him regardless of how he felt. Over time, he regained his sense of spiritual and emotional equilibrium, but it didn't happen overnight.

God's grace was with him in a very special way during that time of shock, and God's presence was with him after the shock wore off—even when he didn't *feel* God's presence. Shock may affect the way we feel. It may temporarily numb our senses, but at no point are we ever removed from God's love or from having His presence in our lives.

Keep in mind that no two people are identical, and no two people's experiences or situations will be identical. However, regardless of how people's personalities or the intensity of their feelings differ, God's love for and desire to help His people are consistent.

---

[1] Alan D. Wolfelt, *Death and Grief: A Guide for Clergy* (Muncie, Ind.: Accelerated Development Inc., 1988), p. 36.

[2] Robert Blair, *The Minister's Funeral Handbook: A Complete Guide to Professional and Compassionate Leadership* (Grand Rapids: Baker Book House Company, 1990), p. 35.

chapter 2

STAGES:
GRIEF RECOVERY IS A PROCESS

"Before losing a loved one, I had thought that there would be a period of deep sadness for a time, and then it would all be over. But for me, there were several distinct emotions that would cycle—shock, disbelief, anger, sadness, tears, calmness, feeling out of control, etc. And then I would feel fine, thinking I was 'finished.' Then the emotions would start over. The most difficult time was about six months after my dad's death."

"I found that recovering from grief is a process, and sometimes it's one step forward and two steps back."

"I felt out of control. Even though I know the Holy Spirit is my Helper and my Comforter, for some time I felt very helpless."

"Mainly I learned that there is a process that you go through whether you want to or not. It doesn't do any good to deny your loss. Everyone deals with separation differently—there is no right or wrong way—don't fear the lack of control because there will come a day when you feel normal again."

PHASES OF RECOVERY

Several authors have made the observation that there are certain phases, or stages, that the bereaved experience following the death of a loved one. It is commonly acknowledged that these phases are not as orderly as the terms might suggest. They are generalizations only and are not meant to be ironclad or rigidly applied. Every person is unique, and though there may be certain common denominators in the grief recovery process, people don't necessarily experience everything on any given list, nor do they progress through these various emotions in an exact, systematic, and orderly fashion.

In his book *Good Grief*, Granger Westberg lists ten components of what people commonly face when significant loss is experienced.

1. Shock
2. The expression of emotion
3. Feelings of depression and loneliness
4. Physical symptoms of distress
5. Feelings of panic
6. Feelings of guilt
7. Feelings of anger and resentment
8. Difficulty in returning to normal activities
9. The gradual resurfacing of hope
10. The establishing of a new reality.[1]

Should we read such a list and assume it is mandatory that every person going through loss must experience each of these? Certainly not—remember, these are descriptions, not *prescriptions*. But a person who has lost a loved one can take comfort if he is encountering some of these described issues. He can find relief in knowing that he is not crazy, abnormal, losing his mind, or weak in faith. He can also find strength in knowing that those particular reactions won't last forever.

Others have used different terminology in attempting to describe the typical process or pattern that people experience in working through grief. Alan D. Wolfelt, a counselor who specializes in working with people recovering from grief, describes three "dimensions" of what people experience following the death of a loved one: evasion, encounter, and reconciliation.

Evasion is described as that phase in which a person is emotionally overwhelmed and endeavors to avoid the painful reality of what has happened. This dimension is marked by shock, denial, numbness, and disbelief.

The encounter dimension occurs when the painful reality of loss sets in and the process of sorting and working through a number of issues begins. Some of the issues a person may face and need to work through at various times during this process include:

- Disorganization, confusion, searching, and yearning.
- Anxiety, panic, and fear.
- Physiological changes (including difficulties with eating and sleeping, as well as diminished energy).
- Explosive emotions.
- Guilt, remorse, and assessing culpability (Culpability deals with blame. Often the surviving person will say, "If only I had . . .").
- Feelings of loss, emptiness, and sadness.
- Feelings of relief and release (These can be especially strong if the deceased suffered before dying. For the bereaved to feel relief or release does not mean that the person who died was not loved. The bereaved can feel this way because their loved one is no longer suffering).

Wolfelt gave the following summary of *reconciliation*—what he described as the final dimension of grief:

> Reconciliation is the dimension wherein the full reality of the death becomes a part of the mourner. Beyond an intellectual working through is an emotional working through. What has been understood at the "head" level is now understood at the "heart" level—the person who was loved is dead. . . .
>
> The pain changes from being ever present, sharp, and stinging to an acknowledged feeling of loss that has given rise to renewed meaning and purpose. The sense of loss does not completely disappear yet softens and the intense pangs of grief become less frequent. Hope for a continued life emerges as the griever is able to make commitments to the future, realizing that the dead person will never be forgotten, yet knowing that one's own life can and will move forward.[2]

Norman Wright, noted author and counselor, depicted recovery in the following way:

> Recovery does not mean a once-and-for-all conclusion to your loss and grief. It is a twofold process involving regaining your ability to function as you once did and resolving and integrating your loss into your life. . . . In a sense, you will never recover completely because you will never be exactly the way you were before. Your loss changes you. . . . Recovery means you get your capabilities and attributes back so you can use them. Part of the process means you are no longer fighting your loss but accepting it. Acceptance doesn't mean you would have chosen it or even that you like it. You have learned to live with it as a part of your life. Recovery doesn't mean you don't mourn occasionally. It means you learn to live with your loss so you can go on with your life . . . . Recovery means reinvesting your life, looking for new relationships and new dreams.[3]

Christians sometimes struggle with the idea that grief recovery is a process that takes time. They will protest, "We are Christians! We know our loved one is in heaven. After all, the Bible says that Christians are not supposed to grieve!"

As much as we would all like automatic exemption from grief, or at least, an immediate and instantaneous recovery from all emotional pain, such desire is based more on wishful thinking than on an accurate understanding of Scripture.

ARE WE TO 'SORROW NOT'?

The Apostle Paul did not command Christians to "sorrow not" as some have suggested. Instead, Paul said, "But I would not have you to be ignorant, brethren, concerning them which are asleep, that ye sorrow not, *even as others which have no hope*"(1 Thessalonians 4:13 *KJV*).

Note again that Paul did not say, "Sorrow not." He didn't tell us not to grieve. He simply said that we are not to grieve *in the same way* that people who have no hope of eternal life or heaven would grieve.

Paul certainly did not denounce all forms of grieving and emotional expression. He told the Romans to weep with those who weep (Romans 12:15). He also told the Philippians that if a certain friend of his had died, he himself would have experienced "sorrow upon sorrow" (Philippians 2:27). Paul did not deny the reality of loss and sorrow, but he affirmed the fact that the believer's experience of loss is one that can and should be infused with divine comfort and hope for the future.

Paul qualified the *nature* and *type* of grief that was to be experienced by believers. It is not the bleak and fatalistic grief experienced by those without hope. Rather, it is a sorrow tempered by the comfort of an anticipated resurrection, by the presence of the Holy Spirit, and by the promises of God's Word.

Obviously, Paul did not believe that Christians would automatically escape all feelings of grief. Shortly after saying, *". . . lest you sorrow as others who have no hope,"* Paul also said, *"Therefore comfort one another with these words"* (1 Thessalonians 4:13,18). If Christians were not to experience any kind of grief whatsoever, and if they were exempt from all sorrow, why would they need to comfort one another? We need to comfort one another, because even as believers we still feel a certain type of sorrow when someone we love is no longer with us.

IS THERE SUCH A THING AS A TIMETABLE?

Even with the hope of heaven, we can still feel elements of sorrow when a loved one dies. As we move through the grief recovery process, we may be tempted to wonder how long the process will take and if there is a timetable for recovery.

Speaking of the knowledge of eternal life, Gary Collins said, "This knowledge is comforting, but it does not eliminate the intense pain of grief and the need for solace." Concerning the duration of the grief recovery process, Collins also said, "Nobody can say how long the mourning process will last. For some it may take only a few weeks or a few months, but studies of widows show that most need at least three or four years to reach stability in their lives. Even then life is never like it was before the loved one died."[4]

Christian counselor Norman Wright provided some generalized information concerning the "pattern of peaks and valleys in grief" that occur over time:

> The pain and grief actually intensify at three months and then gradually subside, but not in a steady fashion. They go up and down. Most people don't need a reminder of the

first-year anniversary of the loss of a loved one. The intensity of grief comes rushing in with pain that rivals the initial feelings of loss. This is why no one should ever tell a person that they should be "over it by now" or "feeling better" at any of these times . . . . Everyone varies, but the average length of time for grief over the loss of a loved one is approximately two years for a natural death. If it was accidental it is three years, suicide death is four years and homicide is five years.[5]

Others specializing in the field of grief recovery state that the most difficult time following the death of a loved one is usually between seven and nine months afterward.[6]

Obviously, timetables will be as varied and unique as the individuals who are grieving. It is wise not to put a time limit for recovery upon yourself, or upon a friend who may be grieving. We can give ourselves time to recover, and we can minister to others with mercy and tenderness regardless of how long their particular recovery takes.

EVENT VERSUS PROCESS

As humans, we would rather have a grief recovery event than a grief recovery process. Who would not want instant and absolute relief, a quick fix, and a cure-all?

I have spoken with a few people who experienced what they described as a very remarkable and speedy recovery following the death of a loved one, but my observations are that most people experience a gradual recovery over time. When relationships were close and strong, the quick recovery is the exception, not the rule.

ONE SIZE DOESN'T FIT ALL

Remember that every individual is unique. Never judge yourself by the experiences (or the expectations) of other people. Even though there may be "averages" or general patterns, you are a distinct human being. Author Alan Wolfelt identified ten factors that influence the uniqueness of the grief recovery process for different individuals:

1. The nature of the relationship with the person who died.
2. The availability, helpfulness, and ability of the person to make use of a social support system.
3. The unique characteristics of the bereaved person.
4. The unique characteristics of the person who died.
5. The nature of the death.
6. The person's religious and cultural history.
7. Other crises or stresses in the person's life.
8. Previous experiences with death.
9. The social expectations based on the sex of the survivor.
10. The ritual or funeral experience.[7]

In considering this list, it becomes obvious that there are more than just a few variables that contribute to the uniqueness of each person's experiences with grief.

WHAT DO YOU DO?

What do you do when you find that you are experiencing recovery in stages, and when you feel as though you sometimes take one step forward and two steps back?

- Find meaningful scriptures that comfort and strengthen you when you face unpleasant emotions. Remember that feelings come and go, but God's Word abides forever.
- Remind yourself that God is good and that He is with you, no matter what you feel. He is faithful to keep His promises.
- Stay involved with other people and with your church. These friends can supply additional support that is vital to your recovery process.

- Be gracious to yourself. Give yourself time. Don't get down on yourself, condemn yourself, or assume there is something wrong with you if you feel like things are out of kilter for a while.
- Find someone who will respect what you're going through and allow you to talk about what you're feeling. A compassionate friend, a pastor, or a counselor may be of great help in this regard.
- Talk to God. Express yourself to Him. Don't be embarrassed or withdraw from Him if there are parts of the process that are especially difficult. He knows what you're going through; He understands and He cares.
- Write. Some people express themselves best in a journal. Much of the Book of Psalms could be considered David's journal. He often described distressing situations and emotions he was experiencing. He also used writing to express his faith. For example, he said, *"Yea, though I walk through the valley of the shadow of death, I will fear no evil; for You are with me; Your rod and Your staff, they comfort me"* (Psalm 23:4). Note that he didn't deny the reality of the situation he was walking through, but he affirmed his faith that God was with him and that God was leading him through the situation.
- Make positive decisions. Negative, overwhelming feelings tend to paralyze people, causing them to withdraw from daily life. It's important to do what you need to do in spite of how you feel. Instead of waiting for your feelings to change, make positive decisions and do the right things, knowing that your feelings will change over time.

Throughout the grief recovery process it will help you to realize that your challenging feelings won't last forever. Remember to talk to yourself in a positive way—a way that is in line with the Scriptures. This is something that David did:

1 SAMUEL 30:6 (*King James Version*)

6 And David was greatly distressed; for the people spake of stoning him, because the soul of all the people was grieved, every man for his sons and for his daughters: but David encouraged himself in the Lord his God.

PSALM 42:11

11 Why are you cast down, O my soul? And why are you disquieted within me? Hope in God; For I shall yet praise Him, The help of my countenance and my God.

PSALM 116:7

7 Return to your rest, O my soul, For the Lord has dealt bountifully with you.

Although negative thoughts and emotions may be present at times, argue against negative and discouraging thoughts by replacing them with thoughts that strengthen and encourage you. Contrary to how you may feel at the moment, you will make it through this grieving process; in the meantime, keep trusting God and putting one foot in front of the other.

---

[1] From GOOD GRIEF by Granger E. Westberg, copyright © 1962, 1971 Fortress Press. Adapted by permission of Augsburg Fortress (www.augsburgfortress.org).

[2] Alan D. Wolfelt, *Death and Grief: A Guide for Clergy* (Muncie, Ind.: Accelerated Development Inc., 1988), pp. 33–61.

[3] H. Norman Wright, *Recovering From the Losses of Life* (Tarrytown, N.Y.: Fleming H. Revell Company, 1991), p. 112.

[4] Reprinted by permission of Thomas Nelson Publishers from the book entitled *Christian Counseling: A Comprehensive Guide* (Revised Edition), copyright 1988 by Gary R. Collins. p. 346–347.

[5] H. Norman Wright, *Crisis Counseling*, copyright 1993, Gospel Light/Regal Books, Ventura., Calif. 93003, pp. 164–165. Used by permission.

[6] Delores Kuenning, *Helping People Through Grief* (Minneapolis: Bethany House Publishers, 1987), p. 219.

[7] Wolfelt, p. 109.

chapter 3

IT'S OKAY TO CRY

"Many Christians said things like, 'Oh, I heard your dad died. Praise the Lord, he's in heaven,' and, 'He was saved, right? Then you don't have anything to be concerned about.' Those comments seemed so insensitive. I know my father was saved, but I still missed him in the natural. Some people forget that we are still human and have emotions. A mere, 'I'm sorry to hear about your dad,' spoken sincerely by non-Christians was more comforting than some of the church things I heard."

One of the major issues encountered in dealing with the death of a loved one pertains to human emotions. Some people have been taught that if a person really has faith, they will not or should not experience any kind of negative emotions following a loved one's death. But is this idea in line with the teaching of the Bible?

Ecclesiastes 3:4 states that there is *"a time to weep, and a time to laugh; a time to mourn, and a time to dance."* Jesus expressed the supportive and consoling nature of God toward those distressed by loss when He said, *"Blessed are those who mourn, for they shall be comforted"* (Matthew 5:4). He certainly did not say, "Shame on those who mourn," or any other condemning words. Jesus also entered fully into the experience of human sorrow when He wept at the tomb of His friend Lazarus (John 11:35).

New Testament believers are seen expressing their grief in Acts 8:2 as "godly men [who] buried Stephen and mourned deeply for him" (*NIV*). The Apostle Paul, a man of great faith, acknowledged his own humanness when he spoke of the fact that his friend, Epaphroditus, had been sick and was very close to death. He stated, *"God had mercy on him, and not only on him but on me also, lest I should have sorrow upon sorrow"* (Philippians 2:27).

The Old Testament also presents several cases of people, even great heroes of faith, expressing their grief and their emotions in an outward and visible way.

- Abraham mourned the death of Sarah and wept for her (Genesis 23:2).

- Jacob mourned many days when he believed his son Joseph had been killed (Genesis 37:34).

- Joseph and others mourned the death of Jacob (Genesis 50:1–13).

- The people of Israel mourned the deaths of Aaron (Numbers 20:29) and Moses (Deuteronomy 34:5–8).

- David mourned the deaths of his infant son (2 Samuel 12:21–23), his adult son, Absalom (2 Samuel 18:33), and the deaths of Jonathon and Saul (2 Samuel 1:11–27).

- Jeremiah and the nation of Israel mourned the death of King Josiah (2 Chronicles 35:23–25).

- Eliphaz, Bildad, and Zophar mourned for Job's adversity (Job 2:11–13).

Lest grieving should be an entirely individual experience isolating the mourner from much needed friendship and support, Paul encouraged believers to weep with those who weep

(Romans 12:15). Yet many people often have a hard time dealing with the issue of emotions.

VARIOUS RESPONSES TO EMOTION

Some people are uncomfortable with their own emotions, and especially uncomfortable around others who may be experiencing emotional turmoil. To avoid personal discomfort, many people simply avoid the bereaved. These people attempt to justify keeping their distance by telling themselves, *They probably just want to be alone.*

Some people tend to be unemotional. They may even believe it is a sign of weakness, especially for men, to express emotions. As a result, they suppress their emotions and are embarrassed to cry or to show sadness. They might feel obligated to "be strong" and show others how much "faith" they have by appearing to be totally victorious.

Other people are at the opposite end of the spectrum. These individuals not only express emotion, but they are continually and perpetually controlled by their feelings. It is understood that a person could feel overcome by a strong emotional reaction, especially following a major loss, but our feelings are not meant to rule us or dominate us on an ongoing and perpetual basis.

In the Book of Psalms, we see David and others honestly express what they felt when they experienced various circumstances and situations. David did not deny the reality of his feelings, but neither did he allow them to rule over him. He poured out his heart before God, and allowed God to help him with and through what he was experiencing.

A perfect example of this is found in First Samuel 30:1–6. In this passage of Scripture, David and his men were out on a military expedition. When they returned, they discovered that their wives, their children, and all of their possessions had been taken, and the town had been burned. In verse 4, we see the reaction of David and his men: *"Then David and the people who were with him lifted up their voices and wept, until they had no more power to weep."*

When emotions are intense, people can be more inclined to make impulsive decisions. Impulsive decisions can cause matters to go from bad to worse. Fortunately, David allowed his faith in God to play a part in how he handled his emotions and in his decision-making. Consider how his situation progressed: *"Now David was greatly distressed, for the people spoke of stoning him, because the soul of all the people was grieved, every man for his sons and his daughters. But David strengthened himself in the Lord his God"* (v. 6).

David demonstrated a healthy balance in this story. He was human enough to have emotions and express them, but when he needed to make a decision to move forward in life, he did so. This same David wrote the famous words, *"Yea, though I walk through the valley of the shadow of death, I will fear no evil; for You are with me; Your rod and Your staff, they comfort me"* (Psalm 23:4). Notice that David did not say he was going to set up camp, or a permanent residence, in the valley of the shadow of death. He said, "Yea, though I walk THROUGH. . . ." A believer must have confidence that God is going to walk him or her through the problem.

FINDING EMOTIONAL EQUILIBRIUM CAN TAKE TIME

This is not to say that emotions can be turned on and off like a light switch. People working through grief have learned that it takes time to process certain emotions. Don't become frustrated and discouraged with yourself if you find that it's taking you longer than you would like. Even though you make decisions and endeavor to live by those decisions, it can still take considerable time before you feel you have regained spiritual and emotional equilibrium following a significant loss.

Consider the following statements made by different individuals:

"I was disturbed when it seemed I couldn't control my emotions. It was a very helpless feeling. I learned to pray and walk through an emotion with God rather than fight or deny the emotion. I accepted this as part of the healing process."

"The whole storm of emotions went beyond anything I had ever experienced, and I wondered if I could possibly deal with them, endure them, and go through them."

"I didn't know a person could go through so many different kinds of emotions and feelings through the recovery process. Going through this has totally changed the way I view life and relationships."

"I did not know the importance of expressing my grief through crying. As a man, I held my emotions in check and would not give vent to my grief. It was actually a couple of months before the impact hit me, and I did get relief through weeping. Now I know it's okay to express our grief."

"The suddenness of emotion was troubling to me. Someone will say something or do something, and it triggers a switch. Then comes a sudden flood . . . a wave of emotion . . . tears suddenly. Christmas was different. I was surprised at how much self-pity I had to battle."

"It helped to learn that the things I was experiencing were normal, healthy expressions of loss, and that in time I would recover. I learned that faith, in the case of losing a loved one, is not meant to shut emotions off. I have learned that everyone's experience and emotions run differently."

How does God feel about the people who experienced these things? Was He mad at them for crying? Was He impatient with them for being emotional? No! He loved them and helped them, the same way He wants to help anyone experiencing distress.

2 CORINTHIANS 1:3–4

3 Blessed be the God and Father of our Lord Jesus Christ, the Father of mercies and God of all comfort,

4 who comforts us in all our tribulation, that we may be able to comfort those who are in any trouble, with the comfort with which we ourselves are comforted by God.

Sometimes, just knowing that you aren't the only one to feel or experience certain things is tremendously helpful. Countless people have become isolated in their thinking, imagining that they were the only ones to ever face or feel what they were experiencing. When people who are struggling with their emotions discover that their feelings are common (see 1 Corinthians 10:13), they often sense great relief. Some people have said, "I'm so glad to find out that what I'm going through is normal; I thought I was losing my mind."

GOD GAVE YOU EMOTIONS

You need to know that God did not create you to be a robot. He gave you emotions, and they have a significant role in your life. God gave you the ability to *feel*—the ability that causes you to feel emotional pain is the same ability that enables you to give and receive joy and love.

God did not create you to be emotionless, but neither did He create you so that emotions and feelings would be the lord of your life. Talk to God about what you're going through. Be honest with Him. Pour out your heart before Him. He's not offended by your emotions, and He wants to walk through this process with you.

HEBREWS 4:15–16

15 For we do not have a High Priest who cannot sympathize with our weaknesses, but was in all points tempted as we are, yet without sin.

16 Let us therefore come boldly to the throne of grace, that we may obtain mercy and find grace to help in time of need.

The good news is that God not only understands your emotional struggles, but He is totally committed to bringing you into a place of joy, gladness, and wholeness—no matter how impossible that may seem to you right now.

Consider these scriptures:

PSALM 30:11

11 You have turned for me my mourning into dancing; You have put off my sackcloth and clothed me with gladness.

ISAIAH 60:20

20 Your sun shall no longer go down, Nor shall your moon withdraw itself; For the Lord will be your everlasting light, And the days of your mourning shall be ended.

The role and assignment of the Messiah is described in Isaiah chapter 61. We read that Jesus came to comfort and console all who mourn, to give them beauty for ashes, the oil of joy for mourning, and the garment of praise for the spirit of heaviness (vv. 2–3).

Sometimes we tend to run away from God when we need Him the most. No matter how you feel right now, turn to God; talk to Him. He is ready and willing to walk with you through whatever experiences you may be facing. He is your very present help in the time of trouble (Psalm 46:1).

chapter 4

COMING TO GRIPS WITH GUILT

Feelings of guilt are some of the most common, pervasive, and troubling emotions with which people deal after the death of a loved one. Consider some of the following comments that different individuals have made:

"*I felt that maybe in some way I had failed her.*"

"*The combination of guilt and regret was really challenging. I longed later to go back and relive those moments and do them differently. I was so sorry for the missed opportunities . . . I had been selfish in several ways . . . I had to repent, learn from my failure, receive God's mercy, and (hardest of all) forgive myself. I had to accept what I could not change and give the devil no place.*"

"*I felt regret over not having spent more time with my grandpa and not having valued the time I did spend with him. I was always in a rush, as he was getting old. My grandma says he knew I loved him, but I guess I've still felt guilt.*"

"*I felt great relief when my mom died. She had been ill for a very long time, and we had watched her slowly deteriorate for many years. I felt much guilt for feeling relieved. It's a strange mix. You exhale relief, but then you gulp in guilt.*"

"*Guilt was the most challenging and troubling emotion I felt after mom's death (I was eight years old). I felt responsible for mom's death for some reason. I wished it had been me instead of her. I felt guilty if I cried, but I felt guilty when I didn't. I felt guilty when I started to love and accept my stepmom. I felt guilty that I didn't tell my mom I loved her before I went to school that morning. I even felt guilty as I grew up when people started saying how much I reminded them of my mom. Guilt literally began to ruin my life."*

"The thing that helped me the most was taking God at His Word: 'Cast all your cares upon Him, for He cares for you' (1 Peter 5:7). I knew I couldn't live the way I was. I was so miserable and wanted to run away or kill myself. So, I took God at His Word and cast all those feelings of guilt onto Him. I prayed that the peace that passes all understanding would guard my heart and my mind in Christ Jesus (Philippians 4:7). For a long time I would wake up every morning and have to do this. Over time, the guilt left and the peace remained."

Experiencing a significant loss can throw us into a state of intensive self-examination. We may begin to critically analyze everything we said and did, as well as everything we *didn't* say or do. Not only can this self-imposed scrutiny be extremely harsh, but it is unfair when we judge ourselves as if our current hindsight had been foresight. For example, if we did not realize that someone was near death, and we did not do something we later wish we had done, we judge ourselves as though we had known he or she was going to die, or at least as though we should have known.

'NORMAL' GUILT VERSUS 'NEUROTIC' GUILT

Granger Westberg differentiates between what he calls "normal guilt" and "neurotic guilt."

An illustration of neurotic guilt might be a daughter who stayed by her aged mother's bedside for days and days without sleep. The doctor now orders her to go home and get some sleep. This turns out to be the night that her mother dies, and she will never forgive herself for not being there when it happened. She broods endlessly about this and builds it up out of proportion to the real situation.[1]

In this situation, no one can fault the daughter for her actions. Neither God nor her mother nor her family and friends would take a judgmental or condemning attitude toward her. Actually, she would be commended for her devotion and her commitment to her mother. However, because of the intensity of her emotional involvement in the situation, her interpretation of her actions may be negatively blown out of proportion in her own mind.

At times, we may judge ourselves with unrealistic expectations, and obviously, we fall short of perfection. When this happens, we feel a sense of guilt, whether or not it is truly merited.

DO WE NEED FORGIVENESS OR REASSURANCE?

If our guilt is a false guilt, or a "neurotic guilt" (a guilt not in proportion to what we did or did not do), then our real need is *reassurance* rather than forgiveness. The Apostle John spoke of times when our own heart may condemn us, and he said that at such times it is appropriate to "assure our hearts before God" (see 1 John 3:19–20). However, if our guilt is based on actual sin and wrongdoing, then we need to ask God for forgiveness, and we also need to forgive ourselves.

Guilt is a normal, healthy response when we have actually done wrong or committed a sin. If we can do wrong and not feel guilty, then our conscience may have become insensitive, callous, or seared. When we experience guilt, the appropriate thing to do is to go to the Lord and see if there is something we genuinely need to repent of and confess as sin.

King David is a biblical example of someone who committed sin. When Nathan the prophet confronted him, this was David's response:

PSALM 51:1–10 (*New Living Translation*)

1 Have mercy on me, O God, because of your unfailing love. Because of your great compassion, blot out the stain of my sins.

2 Wash me clean from my guilt. Purify me from my sin.

3 For I recognize my shameful deeds—they haunt me day and night.

4 Against you, and you alone, have I sinned; I have done what is evil in your sight.
You will be proved right in what you say, and your judgment against me is just.

5 For I was born a sinner—yes, from the moment my mother conceived me.

6 But you desire honesty from the heart, so you can teach me to be wise in my inmost being.

7 Purify me from my sins, and I will be clean; wash me, and I will be whiter than snow.

8 Oh, give me back my joy again; you have broken me—now let me rejoice.

9 Don't keep looking at my sins. Remove the stain of my guilt.

10 Create in me a clean heart, O God. Renew a right spirit within me.

In the New Testament, we are promised that if we confess our sins to God, He is faithful to forgive us. First John 1:9 says, "*If we confess our sins, He is faithful and just to forgive us our sins and to cleanse us from ALL unrighteousness.*" God will not only forgive us for sins of *commission*—when we've done something wrong, but He also forgives us for sins of *omission*—not having done something we should have done (James 4:17).

GODLY SORROW VERSUS
THE SORROW OF THE WORLD

We see another example of godly sorrow, which is an appropriate response to guilt, in the Corinthians' response to Paul's corrective letter:

2 CORINTHIANS 7:8–10

8 For even if I made you sorry with my letter, I do not regret it; though I did regret it. For I perceive that the same epistle made you sorry, though only for a while.

9 Now I rejoice, not that you were made sorry, but that your sorrow led to repentance. For you were made sorry in a godly manner, that you might suffer loss from us in nothing.

10 For GODLY SORROW produces repentance leading to salvation, not to be regretted; but the SORROW OF THE WORLD produces death.

Paul didn't want to just make the Corinthian believers feel bad and wallow in guilt over their wrongdoing. He wanted them to recognize where adjustments were needed, make those corrections, and by God's mercy and grace, receive forgiveness and move forward with their lives. Paul did not desire to see them hanging their heads in shame and living a life of sorrowful remorse. He wanted their lives to be improved by their response to what he wrote.

THE HARDEST PERSON TO FORGIVE

It seems sometimes that the hardest person to forgive is our own self! I have talked with many people who had failed in some area of their life, and they just couldn't seem to forgive themselves. They continually abused themselves, mentally and emotionally speaking. It was as though they felt they had to somehow make themselves miserable for a long time to punish themselves, and to somehow "atone" for the guilt and shame they were feeling over their failure.

I asked these people what their attitude would be had one of their friends made the same mistake toward them—how would they feel about that person, and how would they counsel their friend? Without exception, these people have said that they would forgive their friend and encourage their friend to forgive himself. They would tell their friend to move forward in life and not to let his mistake torment him or hold him back.

After these people explained how they would counsel another in this type of situation, I asked them why they couldn't personally apply and follow the advice they would give to their friend. They were a bit shocked as they realized they were being far harder on themselves than they would have been on a friend.

It seems as though it's easier for us to forgive others than it is for us to forgive ourselves. But the deceased would not want us languishing in guilt and lamenting our remorse either. Our deceased loved ones would recognize that all of us (including them!) have failed and been less than perfect in our relationships. Life is all about grace and mercy—forgiving ourselves and forgiving others.

WE CAN'T CHANGE THE PAST

As difficult as it may be to accept, we cannot go back and relive the past. There are things pertaining to our relationship with those who have died that we simply cannot change. If we now realize that we were not as attentive to or as involved with someone who died as we feel we should have been, we cannot go back and change that.

However, we can make a quality decision to be more appreciative of the friends and family members we still have with us. We can take that lesson, as painful as it might be, and make it a redemptive part of our growth as a human being. However, to continually beat ourselves up over our past mistakes does not help anyone, nor does it change what happened or improve our present situation.

The author of the Serenity Prayer expressed great wisdom when he prayed, "Lord, grant me the serenity to accept the things I cannot change; the courage to change the things I can; and the wisdom to know the difference."

NO LONGER A SLAVE TO GUILT

It may be *natural* to feel guilty, especially when we've done wrong; but it's *supernatural* to receive forgiveness and live in freedom. Consider the following story:

A little boy visiting his grandparents was given his first slingshot. He practiced in the woods, but he could never hit his target.

As he came back to Grandma's back yard, he spied her pet duck. On an impulse he took aim and let fly. The stone hit, and the duck fell dead.

The boy panicked. Desperately he hid the dead duck in the woodpile, only to look up and see his sister watching. Sally had seen it all, but she said nothing.

After lunch that day, Grandma said, "Sally, let's wash the dishes." But Sally said, "Johnny told me he wanted to help in the kitchen today. Didn't you Johnny?" And she whispered to him, "Remember the duck!" So Johnny did the dishes.

Later, Grandpa asked if the children wanted to go fishing. Grandma said, "I'm sorry, but I need Sally to help me make supper." Sally smiled and said, "That's all taken care of. Johnny wants to do it." Again she whispered, "Remember the duck." Johnny stayed while Sally went fishing.

After several days of Johnny doing both his chores and Sally's, finally he couldn't stand it. He confessed to Grandma that he'd killed the duck.

"I know, Johnny," she said, giving him a hug. "I was standing at the window and saw the whole thing. Because I love you, I forgave you. I wondered how long you would let Sally make a slave of you."

We need to ask ourselves the same question when we are struggling with guilt—how long are we going to allow guilt to make a slave of us? Before we were born, God knew every mistake we would ever make and every sin we would ever commit. He still loves us, and He still sent His Son, Jesus, to die for our sins and to take away our guilt and shame. Jesus shed His blood so we could be free, so that we would no longer have to be a slave to guilt, shame, or condemnation.

A PRAYER FOR FORGIVENESS

If you are dealing with guilt over the death of a loved one, pray this prayer:

Dear Heavenly Father,

I come to You right now, realizing that I have fallen short of being the person I would have liked to have been in regards to _____. There are things I didn't say or do that I wish I had said and done, and there are things I said and did that I wish I had not. I did not appreciate or value my time with _____ the way I wish I had, and I am now feeling regret and guilt over all of this.

I ask You to forgive me for areas where I was less than perfect. I thank You that You are merciful and forgiving, and I receive your forgiveness right now. I also ask You to help me as I make the decision right now to forgive myself. I know that You don't want me to go around punishing myself or living under a cloud of guilt.

I also ask You to help me to put this whole situation into perspective. Help me not to judge myself too harshly. I know that hindsight is always 20/20, and I realize that it is unfair to put unrealistic expectations upon others or myself.

Help me to remember the good times, to focus on the positive aspects of the relationship, and to become a better person because of my experiences in life. I am growing, and I thank You for your help in becoming the person You want me to be.

In Jesus' Name I pray. Amen.

Whenever feelings of shame or condemnation try to weigh you down, remember that you prayed this prayer and thank God for setting you free from guilt!

STAYING FREE FROM GUILT

Remember that our feelings can take time to process. Feelings that are unpleasant may try to linger for a season, but we can continue to "feed" and reinforce our decisions based on the Word of God. The more we affirm and positively reinforce our decisions, the stronger that reality will become in our lives.

If feelings of guilt linger, don't cower down and assume you've been unsuccessful. Instead, reinforce your decision by thanking God for and holding fast to your forgiveness no matter how you feel. Feelings can be fickle and subject to change. If thoughts come to you suggesting that you haven't been forgiven, argue against those feelings with the Word of God.

In the *King James Version* of the Bible, Jonah 2:8 says, "They that observe lying vanities forsake their own mercy." The *New International Version* translates the same verse as, "Those who cling to worthless idols forfeit the grace that could be theirs."

Feelings or thoughts that exalt themselves against the Word of God could be said to be idolatrous "lying vanities." Don't "observe" or "cling to" those kinds of thoughts and feelings. We can't necessarily prevent the presentation of such thoughts or feelings, but we don't have to embrace them or entertain them. We can argue against them with the truth of God's Word.

No matter the reason for the guilt—whether we need reassurance or forgiveness—God is present to meet our every need. As we look to Him in times of emotional crisis, be it sorrow, confusion, or guilt, He will comfort and strengthen our heart.

---

[1] From GOOD GRIEF by Granger E. Westberg, copyright © 1962, 1971 Fortress Press. Adapted by permission of Augsburg Fortress (www.augsburgfortress.org), p. 48.

chapter 5

WHY AM I ANGRY?

We have learned that it is okay to grieve and to cry. We even recognize that feelings of sadness and sorrow are legitimate and understandable emotions. But what about feelings of anger? Isn't anger a sin?

Anger is a form of protest. When we consider something to be unfair or unjust, when something (or someone) we value is taken from us, or when we feel threatened, we naturally have an emotional response. Something within us reacts. We may say it out loud or merely feel it within ourselves, but something says, *This is not fair! This is not right! I object! I protest!*

One of the common emotions felt following the death of a loved one is anger. Consider the following statements:

"I was angry at my Dad because he continued making wrong decisions until it ended his life needlessly."

"I was angry . . . angry at myself for not being there for my grandmother; angry that the doctors had let this happen; angry at God for not preventing it from happening."

"I was so hurt. I felt alone. Some time later, the Lord revealed to me that the deep root I felt as the emotion of anger had to do with my mother's death. I realized that I had no right to hold anything against my mom, and I began to

see deep down inside I needed to forgive her. At that moment, I forgave my mom for leaving this earth so soon. Then the Lord had me call someone I trust and confess this. This friend understood and encouraged me in this step of growth."

Many have been trained to believe that anger is undesirable and wrong—that anger is a sin. As a result, many people are not honest with themselves or with others and they seek to hide or repress their anger. They may say the socially appropriate and acceptable words—what they think people expect them to say—and they may "act" properly, but inside they are dealing with anger.

JESUS AND ANGER

While it is true that anger can be acted upon in a way that is sinful, anger in and of itself is not necessarily a sin. We know that Jesus never sinned, and yet He experienced anger. Consider the following passage of Scripture:

MARK 3:1–5

1   And He [Jesus] entered the synagogue again, and a man was there who had a withered hand.

2   So they watched Him closely, whether He would heal him on the Sabbath, so that they might accuse Him.

3   And He said to the man who had the withered hand, "Step forward."

4   Then He said to them, "Is it lawful on the Sabbath to do good or to do evil, to save life or to kill?" But they kept silent.

5   AND WHEN HE HAD LOOKED AROUND AT THEM WITH ANGER, BEING GRIEVED BY THE HARDNESS OF THEIR HEARTS, He said to the man, "Stretch out your hand." And he stretched it out, and his hand was restored as whole as the other.

The Gospel of John gives us another scriptural incident in which Jesus was obviously angry.

JOHN 2:13–17

13 Now the Passover of the Jews was at hand, and Jesus went up to Jerusalem.

14 And He found in the temple those who sold oxen and sheep and doves, and the moneychangers doing business.

15 When He had made a whip of cords, He drove them all out of the temple, with the sheep and the oxen, and poured out the changers' money and overturned the tables.

16 And He said to those who sold doves, "Take these things away! Do not make My Father's house a house of merchandise!"

17 Then His disciples remembered that it was written, "Zeal for Your house has eaten Me up."

In Matthew's account of this passage, what happened *after* Jesus' display of anger is most significant. Matthew 21:14 says, *"Then the blind and the lame came to Him in the temple, and He healed them."*

In both of these instances (the healing of the man on the Sabbath and the cleansing of the temple) Jesus felt an emotion that we typically classify as negative, but He ultimately acted in a way that was positive and productive. Jesus was not overcome by the negativity of the situation; instead, He acted redemptively in these situations and caused good to come from them.

As Dr. David Seamands once said:

> Anger is a divinely implanted emotion. Closely allied to our instinct for right, it is designed—as are all our emotions—to be used for constructive spiritual purposes. The person who cannot feel anger at evil is a person who lacks enthusiasm for good. If you cannot hate the wrong, it's very questionable whether you really love righteousness."[1]

41

THE APOSTLE PAUL ON ANGER

The Apostle Paul (a man who definitely experienced anger in his life) made several powerful statements about this intense emotional force.

EPHESIANS 4:26–27,30–32

26 "Be angry, and do not sin": do not let the sun go down on your wrath,

27 nor give place to the devil. . . .

30 And do not grieve the Holy Spirit of God, by whom you were sealed for the day of redemption.

31 Let all bitterness, wrath, anger, clamor, and evil speaking be put away from you, with all malice.

32 And be kind to one another, tenderhearted, forgiving one another, just as God in Christ forgave you.

The *New Living Translation* of Ephesians 4:26 and 27 says, "And 'don't sin by letting anger gain control over you.' Don't let the sun go down while you are still angry, for anger gives a mighty foothold to the Devil."

In examining these verses, it becomes obvious that one can experience the emotion of anger without engaging in sinful behavior. We don't have to allow the wound we've experienced to become infected, thus causing us to act sinfully. Nor does the emotion have to control us or become the focal point of our lives.

The emotion of anger can be aimed in numerous directions. Sometimes people are angry at God for "allowing" something to happen to a loved one. In other cases, the anger is targeted at the person who died. A person can also be angry at people who endeavor to offer words of comfort. Sometimes the anger is seemingly directed at everyone!

'I'M GOING TO SCREAM!'

A widow expressed her anger about the fact that people repeatedly told her that her husband was in heaven with Jesus. Even though they were trying to be helpful, the would-be comforters did not realize that their words were affecting her the wrong way. She said, "If one more person tells me that my husband is with Jesus, I'm going to scream! I know he's with Jesus, and I know he's experiencing the wonders of heaven. But I'm not! I'm stuck down here with all the bills and all the problems that are left behind.

"I know I should be glad for him, but I'm really mad that he's getting to enjoy all the glory of heaven, while I'm stuck down here having to struggle through all the problems of earth. How could he abandon me like this? I needed him so much, and now he's gone. I'm so angry at him, and then I feel guilty for being angry. I know what I'm experiencing is totally selfish, but I'm very overwhelmed with everything right now."

When we're hurting, we can say things that don't reflect our best. This woman was speaking out of great emotional pain. She realized she was being selfish, but at the same time, she was facing a massive adjustment in her life, and it was obviously a great challenge for her to work through all of the transition issues.

She really didn't need to be criticized and corrected at that point. Rather, her situation called for a supportive friend to encourage her as she dealt with this overwhelming time of change in her life and as she worked through her anger. She needed someone to love and accept her in spite of her less-than-pleasant feelings, and gently guide her "back on track" as she recovered from her pain and distress in the matter.

In helping people through these types of situations, it is important not to be easily offended when people make statements that aren't "full of grace." When people are experiencing great grief or distress, their normal judgment and abilities can be significantly impaired. Perhaps this is why writings in the Jewish Talmud indicate that a grieving person should not be held entirely responsible for his or her actions, especially immediately after the loss.[2] Ultimately, we all need to be responsible for our decisions, our attitudes, our words, and our actions. But at the same time, we should offer mercy and not be offended when we realize people are speaking out of great anguish.

JOB LASHED OUT IN ANGER

Job was a righteous man who experienced devastating loss. His children were killed, his vast economic empire was decimated, and his health deteriorated terribly. Out of deep emotional distress, Job lashed out against his three friends and against God.

It is important to remember that Job had no Bible to turn to for answers. He had no way of knowing that it was Satan who had attacked him; he felt it was God who had brought devastation into his life, and he was angry about it. Job perceived all of his woes as a great injustice.

Further, Job's three "friends" who came with the intention of comforting him reacted strongly against his outbursts, condemning him, and telling him (incorrectly) that all the problems he experienced were the result of sin in his life. Consider some of Job's reactionary statements found in the Book of Job:

JOB 7:11

11 Therefore I will not restrain my mouth; I will speak in the anguish of my spirit; I will complain in the bitterness of my soul.

JOB 10:1

1 My soul loathes my life; I will give free course to my complaint, I will speak in the bitterness of my soul.

JOB 13:2–5

2 What you know, I also know; I am not inferior to you.
3 But I would speak to the Almighty, And I desire to reason with God.
4 But you forgers of lies, You are all worthless physicians.
5 Oh, that you would be silent, And it would be your wisdom!

JOB 16:2

2 I have heard many such things; miserable comforters are you all!

No one would dispute the fact that Job had become an angry man! However, much later in the story, when Job finally received a revelation about who God really was, he repented for many of the things he had said (Job 40:4–5; 42:3–6).

Even though God had described Job as a righteous man, Job had to overcome his sense of self-righteousness and commit himself entirely to the care and keeping of God (Job 32:2; 40:8). Job did not experience his initial crisis because of anger, but his anger seemed to be a part of what kept him from receiving the blessing of restoration that God intended for him.

JOB 42:10

10 And the Lord restored Job's losses when he prayed for his friends. Indeed the Lord gave Job twice as much as he had before.

Notice that God's blessings of restoration flowed into Job's life when he took a positive step to move beyond the intense anger he felt toward his friends.

DOES INJUSTICE DESERVE FORGIVENESS?

Anger can be especially intense when a great injustice has occurred. Consider a scenario where a godly, responsible, innocent person is killed by a drunk driver, in a robbery, or as an act of terrorism. Perhaps the drunk driver lives, or the perpetrator of the crime walks away unpunished. Whether the taking of life was unintentional or intentional, it just isn't fair that an innocent person was killed!

When someone we love is killed, it is not unusual for us as survivors to feel an enormous amount of outrage. Not only was someone precious to us killed, but we feel personally violated in the matter. It wasn't just an attack on the person who died; it was an attack upon us as well. Everything that relationship meant to us has also received a massive blow! Our personal needs that were met by that loved one aren't going to be met by him or her any longer. It may seem that our own sense of safety and security has been ripped away, and we wonder, *How could someone do this—not just to my loved one who was killed—but to me, to us?*

It is difficult to reconcile seemingly contradictory facts. However, the truth is that *God is good and life is unfair.* As challenging as it is to embrace both of those truths, they are nonetheless realities of our existence. To not believe that God is good would leave us cynical and cold, without hope and comfort; to not realize that life is unfair—at least in the temporal sense—would leave us naive and ill-prepared to face the challenges of life.

JESUS' PERSONAL REACTION
TO A GREAT INJUSTICE

The gospels tell the story of the murder of John the Baptist, a righteous preacher and cousin of Jesus. John had spoken against the adulterous relationship of Herod and his brother's wife. Motivated by vindictiveness and malice, she arranged for her daughter to dance for Herod at his birthday party. He was so pleased that he promised her whatever she wanted. Prompted by her evil mother, she asked for the head of John the Baptist on a platter. Herod regretted his promise, but because he wanted to preserve his image—he didn't want to look bad to the guests in front of whom he'd made the promise—he issued the necessary orders, and a prophet of God was senselessly murdered.

How did Jesus react when He heard about this? According to Matthew 14:13, "As soon as Jesus heard the news, he went off by himself in a boat to a remote area to be alone" (*New Living Translation*). Was Jesus hurting at this point? Did His heart cry out to His Father because of the injustice? I believe so. And yet Herod, along with you and I, was one for whom Jesus in His great love would eventually die. It's important to know that Jesus went through this kind of tragic situation Himself, and we can be assured that He is fully capable of helping us no matter what we face. He has been there, and He knows how to help us through it.

THE POWER OF FORGIVENESS

Some people are hurting so badly after a tragedy that they don't even want to hear about forgiveness. I am convinced that many people, even believers, have a great misunderstanding of forgiveness. In order to properly understand what forgiveness is, it is vital to understand what forgiveness is not.

- **Forgiveness is not condoning or approving of an evil action. Forgiveness is not saying, "What you did is acceptable."** If what was done was acceptable, no forgiveness would be necessary.

- **Forgiveness does not mean that you place yourself in a position to be continually hurt or abused.** The Apostle Paul said, "*Alexander the coppersmith did me much harm. May the Lord repay him according to his works. You also must beware of him . . .*" (2 Timothy 4:14–15). No doubt Paul forgave Alexander, but he didn't want Timothy to naively place himself in harm's way.

- **Forgiveness is not amnesia.** It is absolutely necessary that we qualify and clarify what is meant when people say that Christians ought to "forgive and forget." Our minds were created with the capability to mentally remember and recall. Forgetting does not mean we lack the ability to mentally recall an event or offense. When we encourage people to "forget the past," we literally mean for people not to let the events of the past dominate their present or dictate their future. We are advising people to not allow themselves to be frozen in time by an event or offense. Life moves forward, and we must move forward also. When we "forget" we move beyond being obsessed with the past event, choosing not to live in reactionary rage to what happened.

- **Forgiveness is not the same as reconciliation.** Reconciliation requires repentance on the part of the offender so that a relationship can be restored. However, we can forgive a person who has offended us whether or not they are repentant.

- **Forgiveness does not necessarily result in the immediate cessation of all unpleasant feelings.** As much as we would like our feelings and emotions to reflect our decisions immediately and absolutely, that is not the case in most situations. The devil often tries to take advantage of people in this area. For example, when a person has been hurt, but he makes the decision to forgive, he may still have some unpleasant feelings for a season. The devil then brings such thoughts as, *You didn't forgive that person—you are a lousy Christian.* When a believer agrees with the devil in this regard and concludes that he didn't forgive, he becomes double-minded in the situation. Instead, he should say, "No, devil. I did forgive that person. The fact that my feelings are still tender is only indicative of the fact that I am human and have emotions. However, I don't live by my emotions; I live by my decisions. I chose to forgive that person, and my feelings will get in line."

In an article in *Guideposts*, Holocaust survivor Corrie ten Boom told of not being able to forget a wrong that had been done to her. She had forgiven those who had hurt her, but she kept rehashing the incident and couldn't sleep. Finally Corrie cried out to God for help in putting the problem to rest. She writes:

> His help came in the form of a kindly Lutheran pastor to whom I confessed my failure after two sleepless weeks. "Up in that church tower," he said, nodding out the window, "is a bell which is rung by pulling on a rope. But you know what? After the sexton lets go of the rope, the bell keeps on swinging. First ding, then dong. Slower and slower until there's a final dong and it stops.
>
> "I believe the same thing is true of forgiveness. When we forgive, we take our hand off the rope. But if we've been tugging at our grievances for a long time, we mustn't be surprised if the old angry thoughts keep coming for a while. They're just the ding-dongs of the old bell slowing down."
>
> And so it proved to be. There were a few more midnight reverberations, a couple of dings when the subject came up in my conversations. But the force—which was my willingness in the matter—had gone out of them. They came less and less often and at last stopped altogether. And so I discovered another secret of forgiveness: we can trust our God not only above our emotions, but also above our thoughts.[3]

We really don't engage in forgiveness for the benefit of the person who committed the wrong against us. We forgive so that we ourselves don't become a perpetual victim of the wrong. We may have been a victim once—the person we loved is no longer with us, and in some ways, our life is forever changed. However, to hold unforgiveness against someone is to allow that offense to continue to plague our life. We can't bring our loved one back, but we do not have to let the offense continue to torment us and be an incessant extension of the original loss.

Forgiveness is our way of releasing the bitterness, resentment, hostility, and rage that would perpetually hold us captive. When you forgive another person, the person you are really liberating is *yourself*.

WHAT THE APOSTLE JAMES SAID ABOUT ANGER

The Bible records Jesus' and the Apostle Paul's dealings with anger. We also know from God's Word what the Apostle James had to say on the subject.

JAMES 1:19–20 (*New International Version*)
19 My dear brothers, take note of this: Everyone should be quick to listen, slow to speak and slow to become angry,
20 for man's anger does not bring about the righteous life that God desires.

The *Beck* translation of verse 20 says, "An angry man doesn't do what's right before God."

We would do well to develop the fruit of the Spirit in our lives in such a way that we are truly quick to listen, slow to speak, and slow to anger. What do these three attributes mean for our practical living? It means that we are ever ready to listen to God's Word. He will instruct us on how we are to respond to the challenges we face in life. It means that we are not quick to just "let fly" whatever words come to mind. Very often, the more impulsively we speak, the more we have to repent for later. Further, we do not benefit anyone, including ourselves, when we are quick to react in a carnal way.

If you are angry right now over a loss you've experienced, let me encourage you to be quick to listen to God's Word. Search His Word to find the comfort and encouragement He has for you. Discover in His Word how He wants you to conduct yourself. Also, be slow to lash out against people.

If you're acting out your anger in a sinful way, the righteous life that God intends for you cannot reach the fullness He desires. This doesn't mean that God is mad at you if you are experiencing anger. On the contrary, He wants to help you. It is one thing to experience an emotion. It is another thing to base your life, your decisions, your conversation, and your actions on that emotion.

When it seems as though your whole world has been unfairly turned upside down, or when it seems as though your sense of security and your hopes and dreams have been ripped from you, working through feelings of anger can be a great challenge. However, with God's help it is possible—and God *does* want to help you.

STEPS TO OVERCOMING ANGER

What are some practical steps you can take to overcome this kind of anger?

1. Talk to God about what you're going through.

Sometimes we tend to *resist* God the most when we *need* Him the most. We must remember that God is not our problem; He is our answer. If we are angry, even if we're angry with God, He still wants to help us. If we believe that the anger we're dealing with has gotten us into sin, then we must confess that to Him and ask Him to forgive us. He will! Further, He not only wants to help us after we've sinned, but if we will go to Him, He will help us avoid ever getting into sin!

> **HEBREWS 4:14–16** (*New Living Translation*)
> 14 That is why we have a great High Priest who has gone to heaven, Jesus the Son of God. Let us cling to him and never stop trusting him.
> 15 This High Priest of ours understands our weaknesses, for he faced all of the same temptations we do, yet he did not sin.
> 16 So let us come boldly to the throne of our gracious God. There we will receive his mercy, and we will find grace to help us when we need it.

Whenever we need help with anger or any other emotion or difficulty, God's grace and mercy are ever available to us.

2. Identify and express your anger in a constructive manner.

There are situations when people are in total denial about their anger. Refusing to admit you are angry (if you really are) does not solve anything. Ephesians 5:13 says, "But when anything is exposed and reproved by the light, it is made visible and clear; and where everything is visible and clear there is light" (*AMP*). If we want clarity of vision and for our path to be illuminated, it is important to be specific in identifying what we are angry about.

3. Conduct an inventory of your thought life. Get your thinking in line with God's Word.

While anger can be a normal reaction to loss, we can either tell ourselves things to aggravate and perpetuate our anger, or we can tell ourselves things to help defuse our anger and help us move beyond it. For example, you can tell yourself:

- *I will never be happy again. I will never recover from this loss.*

- *I will never be able to forgive So-and-so.*

- *My entire purpose in living is gone. I have no future.*

- *I can't make it without So-and-so. God obviously has forsaken me and abandoned me; I'll never trust Him again.*

Can you see how meditating on these types of thoughts can fuel and perpetuate not only anger but also a number of other unhealthy feelings? Even though they may seem very strong, it is important to identify such thoughts (or "self-talk") as lies, argue against them, and replace them with truths from God's Word. Consider telling yourself the following types of statements instead of those we just listed:

- *In spite of how I feel right now, I believe that my God is a restoring God. I believe my sorrow can be turned to joy [Isaiah 35:10; 61:3, John 16:19–22].*

- *God never asks us in His Word to do something that He does not provide us the grace to do. If He commands me to forgive, then He will give me the grace to do so. I make the decision to forgive, and I thank God that He gives me the strength to obey Him.*

- *This situation may have caught me by surprise, but it did not surprise God. He knew me before the foundation of the world, and He established a purpose for my life. He still has good plans for me, and I believe that God is going to help me find new meaning and new purpose for my life.*

- *I will miss So-and-so deeply, but the Lord is still with me, and He has promised to meet all of my needs. With His help, I can and will make it. These are certainly not the circumstances I would have chosen, but in spite of how unfair life seems, I know that God is still good and still faithful. I choose to trust the Lord in spite of this situation.*

4. Establish a discipline of feeding your positive decisions and acting upon them.

A negative thought or feeling doesn't cease to exist or discontinue presenting itself to us simply because we argue against it one time. Many people find it helpful to write down their decisions and the "replacement thoughts" based on God's Word and rehearse them regularly. It is also important to make sure that our actions, as well as our thoughts, are in line with God's Word. Again, this sometimes means making ourselves do things that we don't feel like doing. For example, we may feel like not being around people at certain times. Occasional solitude can be fine, but there comes a point where excessively isolating ourselves is unhealthy. As a result, some people may need to push themselves to stay involved in church, stay involved with friends, and so forth.

This is all part of moving forward with our life. Again, the more we feed our decisions, the stronger they will grow. The more we act upon our positive beliefs in God's Word, the stronger we will become in them. Anger is an issue that all of us have to deal with at one time or another, but with God's help, we can successfully work through and move beyond the anger issues in our life.

---

[1] Dr. David A. Seamands, *Putting Away Childish Things: Reaching for Spiritual and Emotional Maturity in Christ* (Indianapolis: Light and Life Communications, 1999), p. 45.

[2] Alfred J. Kolatch, *The Jewish Mourner's Book of Why* (Middle Village, N.Y.: Johnathan David Publishers, 1993), p. 24.

[3] Reprinted with permission from *Guideposts magazine.* Copyright © 1972 by Guideposts. All rights reserved. www.guidepostsmag.com

chapter 6

ADJUSTING TO THE NEW REALITY

Whenever we lose a loved one, we are forced to make many adjustments. While some adjustments are practical and external, others are emotional and internal. Some may seem trivial—others monumental. Any and every adjustment can be difficult to make, simply because change itself is difficult.

It has often been said that human beings are creatures of habit. We prefer to "live, move, and have our being" in our comfort zone. We arrange and situate our life until we're comfortable, then we like for everything to stay put. We don't want anyone upsetting the apple cart or ruffling our feathers, so to speak. Just the fact that there are so many clichés with reference to this tendency of human nature shows how much we don't like change.

Although we would rather the world be a peaceful, tranquil place, we must come to terms with the fact that there is a great deal of pain and turmoil in the world. There is a part of us that wants to stay young, and we sometimes hear people longing for the good old days. In reality we must all deal with the truth that "our outward man is perishing" (2 Corinthians 4:16). We may have idealistic dreams of the way we wish things could be, but, ultimately, we must face the realities of life.

WHY CAN'T THINGS JUST STAY THE WAY THEY ARE?

When things are going well, it is only natural to want them to stay just as they are. Peter, James, and John often felt this way—once, when Jesus shared a wonderful experience (now called The Transfiguration) with them. Jesus took these three disciples to a mountaintop, where they saw Moses and Elijah talking with Jesus. It was an outstanding event, and Peter did not want to see it come to an end.

LUKE 9:33

33 Then it happened, as they were parting from Him, that Peter said to Jesus, "Master, it is good for us to be here; and let us make three tabernacles: one for You, one for Moses, and one for Elijah"—not knowing what he said.

Peter enjoyed himself so much that he didn't want the experience to end. He wasn't the only person to have felt this way. When Jesus told His disciples that He would die and no longer be with them (in the physical sense), they had great difficulty seeing beyond that transition. They were used to being with Jesus, and it was difficult for them to imagine life without Him at their side (see John 16:5–7). Obviously, Jesus' death and the coming of the Holy Spirit was a unique situation, but the fact remains that we as humans do not like change—especially if it means that someone we love is no longer going to be with us.

EVERYTHING CHANGES

Although we do not like or embrace change, it is wise for us to realize that everything pertaining to this earthly realm is subject to change whether we like it or not. Psalm 102:25 and 26 says, *"Of old You laid the foundation of the earth, and the* [physical] *heavens are the work of Your hands. They will perish, but You will endure; yes, they will all grow old like a garment; like a cloak You will change them, and they will be changed."*

The Old Testament heroes of faith described in Hebrews chapter 11 had learned that this world and everything in it is only temporary. These men and women acknowledged *". . . that they were strangers and pilgrims on the earth. For those who say such things declare plainly that they seek a homeland. And truly if they had called to mind that country from which they had come out, they would have had opportunity to return. But now they desire a better, that is, a heavenly country. Therefore God is not ashamed to be called their God, for He has prepared a city for them"* (Hebrews 11:13–16).

None of our relationships on this earth are permanent, because some of us will leave this earth sooner than others. Thank God for the fact that we can be reunited in heaven, but in the meantime, we must remember that we are truly just "passing through."

In spite of the very transitory nature of life, we become comfortable having things a certain way. When circumstances change, we can have a challenging time dealing with it. This is true in dealing with the death of a loved one and concerning any kind of change. Transitions are a part of life, and we often experience a certain level of stress when:

- We go to a new school.
- We change jobs.
- We move to a new community or into a new house.
- Our children move out of the home.
- We retire.

Some transitions are easier to handle than others. When it comes to having a loved one die, there is usually so much more involved than just the fact that the person is no longer with us. The added issues make the transition a very difficult one to make.

IT IS WELL WITH MY SOUL

When peace, like a river, attendeth my way,
When sorrows like sea billows roll;
Whatever my lot, Thou hast taught me to say,
It is well, it is well with my soul.
Though Satan should buffet, tho' trials should come,
Let this blest assurance control,
That Christ has regarded my helpless estate,
And hath shed His own blood for my soul.
My sin oh, the bliss of this glorious tho't:
My sin not in part, but the whole
Is nail'd to the cross and I bear it no more,
Praise the Lord, praise the Lord, O my soul!
And, Lord, haste the day when my faith shall be sight,
The clouds be roll'd back as a scroll,
The trump shall resound and the Lord shall descend,
"Even so," it is well with my soul.

For years, Christians have been comforted by the hymn "It Is Well With My Soul." Many, though, have been unaware of the circumstances surrounding the writing of this great song.

Some months prior to the Chicago Fire of 1871, [Horatio] Spafford had invested heavily in real estate on the shore of Lake Michigan, and his holdings were wiped out by this disaster. Just before this he had experienced the death of his son. Desiring a rest for his wife and four daughters as well as wishing to join and assist Moody and Sankey in one of their campaigns in Great Britain, Spafford planned a European trip for his family in 1873.

In November of that year, due to unexpected last minute business developments, he had to remain in Chicago; but he sent his wife and four daughters on ahead as scheduled on the S.S. Ville du Havre. He expected to follow in a few days. On November 22 the ship was struck by the Lochearn, an English vessel, and sank in twelve minutes. Several days later the survivors were finally landed at Cardiff, Wales, and Mrs. Spafford cabled her husband, "Saved alone."

Shortly afterward Spafford left by ship to join his bereaved wife. It is speculated that on the sea near the area where it was thought his four daughters had drowned, Spafford penned this text with words so significantly describing his own personal grief—"When sorrows like sea billows roll . . ."

It is noteworthy, however, that Spafford does not dwell on the theme of life's sorrows and trials but focuses attention in the third stanza on the redemptive work of Christ and in the fourth verse anticipates His glorious second coming.

Humanly speaking, it is amazing that one could experience such personal tragedies and sorrows as did Horatio Spafford and still be able to say with such convincing clarity, "It is well with my soul."[1]

DEPENDENCY ISSUES

For example, there are *dependency issues*—how much did we depend upon that person, and how much did he or she depend upon us? What role did he or she play in our life? Perhaps we found a great sense of self-worth in caring for that person and now he or she is no longer with us. Will we find a sense of worth and purpose elsewhere, or will we feel as though we no longer have value?

Perhaps the person was proficient in certain areas—such as managing the finances—so we totally allowed him or her to take care of us in those areas. We may have become completely dependent upon our loved one, completely leaning upon his or her skills. Suddenly, we find ourselves not only without that person, but we encounter new responsibilities for which we may feel very inadequate and unprepared.

In the following statements, you can sense the struggle that is encountered as the grieving adjust to the new reality of living without their loved one:

"The most challenging aspect of dealing with the loss of my husband was learning to live without him. Just as it took time for us to 'become one,' it took time for us to un-become one. The only way I knew to face this was to cry out to God, asking Him to help me and to fill the emptiness of my heart."

"I was not prepared to do all the things my husband had done. With each new challenge came a feeling of being overwhelmed."

"I learned that it takes a long time to adjust to the loss, especially when there is unfinished business with that family member."

IDENTITY ISSUES

When adjusting to the new reality after suffering the loss of a loved one, there may be dependency issues and there may also be *identity issues*. Perhaps our goals and dreams were wrapped up in our loved one—and now that person is gone! Will all of our hopes and aspirations die with our loved one, or will we be able to discover new purpose and new direction in life? Sometimes the loss is so drastic and so devastating that it seems there is no possible way we can go on.

"The most troubling emotion I faced was feeling like I couldn't function as a person any longer. I didn't necessarily want to die, but I felt like I just didn't want to go on with my life."

"I seriously questioned if I would ever feel normal again, and if life would ever be worth living again. It was quite some time before I could say with confidence, 'Yes!'"

"Time truly is great medicine for dealing with grief. At first, I couldn't imagine ever getting over my grandmother's death. Eventually, though, I realized that God had used time to help me heal and live my life."

"It is possible to go on with life, even though it hurts so badly at times. You think you're never going to make it through, but you end up laughing and loving again."

"For some time the feeling that I would never have joy again was very strong."

COMPANIONSHIP ISSUES

In addition to dependency and identity issues, there are also *companionship issues.* It is normal to miss someone when we are no longer able to enjoy his or her physical presence and company. I remember contacting a middle-aged man whose elderly father had just died. When I asked him how he was doing, he gave a very honest answer. He said, "I'm glad my dad is with Jesus and that he's not suffering anymore, but I sure do miss him."

Loneliness is commonly encountered when a loved one dies. Depending on the nature of the relationship, feelings of loneliness can be very intense.

"The feeling of emptiness inside was extremely difficult to deal with, and the feeling of being powerless to reverse the reality of his death."

"I felt extremely lonely and completely hopeless."

"The loneliness I felt because she just wasn't there anymore was overwhelming. For a few days after she left, I imagined I could still hear her footsteps in the house as it used to be when she was with me."

"The thing that stood out to me the most throughout my grieving time was the void, the huge void I felt. My father and I were very close. He called me often and we would talk. He would listen to me for hours. Now the calls from him are gone, and there is just no one who stands in my corner the way my dad did."

"The most troubling feeling was the vast emptiness inside. It was like a big black hole inside of me that got so big at times I could not take it. I thought it would swallow me up."

"The one person I knew who loved me unconditionally was gone. There was such pain that I physically hurt for days."

"I didn't know how to fill the hole, the void that his absence left in my heart."

Don't be alarmed if you have strong feelings of loneliness when someone you love very dearly is separated from you. Just as God gave you the gift of being able to give love to that person and receive love from that person, God will also give you strength and resiliency to move forward. The aching void you feel in your heart is a testimony to the quality of love that God allowed you to share with that individual. Although your loved one is gone, God is still with you, and He will never leave you or forsake you.

It is important for you to believe that God still has a purpose and a reason for you to be alive on this earth. There will never be an exact replica of what you had with your loved one, but you must believe that God still has good things for you in life and that He will help you adjust to your new reality.

A LOOK AT KING DAVID'S RECOVERY

As recorded in the Bible, David faced a very unpleasant transition in his life. Actually, David experienced numerous losses, and one of them involved the death of his child. In this particular incident, the son born out of David's and Bathsheba's adulterous relationship became sick and died. (I want to stress again that by no means is every sickness or death related to a specific sin someone has committed. As we address later in chapter 10, there are numerous reasons why problems can occur.) What I want to focus on in this story is not the cause of the problem, but rather the way in which David responded to his loss.

2 SAMUEL 12:16–23

16 David therefore pleaded with God for the child, and David fasted and went in and lay all night on the ground.

17 So the elders of his house arose and went to him, to raise him up from the ground. But he would not, nor did he eat food with them.

18 Then on the seventh day it came to pass that the child died. And the servants of David were afraid to tell him that the child was dead. For they said, "Indeed, while the child was alive, we spoke to him, and he would not heed our voice. How can we tell him that the child is dead? He may do some harm!"

19 When David saw that his servants were whispering, David perceived that the child was dead. Therefore David said to his servants, "Is the child dead?" And they said, "He is dead."

20 So David arose from the ground, washed and anointed himself, and changed his clothes; and he went into the house of the Lord and worshiped. Then he went to his own house; and when he requested, they set food before him, and he ate.

21 Then his servants said to him, "What is this that you have done? You fasted and wept for the child while he was alive, but when the child died, you arose and ate food."

22 And he said, "While the child was alive, I fasted and wept; for I said, 'Who can tell whether the Lord will be gracious to me, that the child may live?'

23 "But now he is dead; why should I fast? Can I bring him back again? I shall go to him, but he shall not return to me."

Examining this passage of Scripture, let us consider what David did in response to the loss of his son. Let us also recognize what his example might mean for us as we experience the loss of a loved one.

David prayed, fasted, wept, and sought God in the situation (vv. 16–18). In the final analysis, though, David did not receive the outcome he desired. This situation is somewhat unique because the prophet Nathan had already told David that the child was going to die (2 Samuel 12:14). No doubt there was a part of David that did not want to accept what had been revealed through Nathan. There is a part of us that does not want to accept bad news, and perhaps some of David's weeping was a form of what has been called "anticipatory grief." Often people express some of their grieving before the loved one actually dies.

Essentially, David had "pushed every button and pulled every lever" in trying to turn the situation around. David's distress was so great that his advisors were afraid to break the news to him about the death of his son. They had seen how terribly agonized David was while his child was sick, and they feared he might harm himself when he learned of his son's death.

David forced himself to accept news he did not want to hear (v. 19). When David perceived his advisors whispering, he inquired of them and received confirmation that his son had died.

A miserable looking woman recognized F. B. Meyer on the train and ventured to share her burden with him. For years she had cared for a crippled daughter who brought great joy to her life. She made tea for her each morning, then left for work, knowing that in the evening the daughter would be there when she arrived home.

But the daughter had died, and the grieving mother was alone and miserable. Home was not "home" anymore.

Meyer gave her wise counsel.

"When you get home and put the key in the door," he said, "say aloud, 'Jesus, I know You are here!' and be ready to greet Him directly when you open the door. And as you light the fire tell Him what has happened during the day; if anybody has been kind, tell Him; if anybody has been unkind, tell Him, just as you would have told your daughter. At night, stretch out your hand in the darkness and say, 'Jesus, I know You are here!'"

Some months later, Meyer was back in that neighborhood and met the woman again, but he did not recognize her. Her face radiated joy instead of announcing misery. "I did as you told me," she said, "and it has made all the difference in my life, and now I feel I know Him."[2]

David arose from the ground (v. 20). No doubt this literally took place, since David had been lying prostrate before the Lord, but I believe there is powerful imagery included in this statement as well. Sometimes in life, we get *knocked* down. However, we have to decide whether or not we are going to stay down.

The Apostle Paul said, "But this precious treasure—this light and power that now shine within us—is held in perishable containers, that is, in our weak bodies. So everyone can see that our glorious power is from God and is not our own. We are pressed on every side by troubles, but we are not crushed and broken. We are perplexed, but we don't give up and quit. We are hunted down, but God never abandons us. We get knocked down, but we get up again and keep going" (2 Corinthians 4:7–9 *NLT*). Paul was resilient throughout his many trials because he trusted in and relied upon God's strength.

David washed (v. 20). Again, the literal meaning of this phrase applies. However, there is also figurative richness here. Washing has to do with getting rid of yesterday's grime and receiving a fresh start today. Washing has to do with cleansing, refreshing, renewing, and embracing a new beginning. In Ephesians 5:25 and 26, Paul describes Jesus loving, nurturing, and cherishing the Church and giving Himself for her. Paul goes on to write, *"That He might sanctify and cleanse her with the washing of water by the word"* (v. 26). There is a washing that comes from receiving the Word of God, and that washing cleanses us from the doubts, fears, and confusion that occur during times of great loss.

David anointed himself (v. 20). In addition to being a symbol of the Holy Spirit, oil had a myriad of practical uses in Bible days. It was a lotion and a moisturizer that brought comfort, refreshing, and relief to a person. Oil was nourishing and soothing and was used to treat bodily injuries. Perhaps the best known verse in the Old Testament about anointing with oil was written by David himself when he said, *"You anoint my head with oil; My cup runs over"* (Psalm 23:5).

David changed his clothes (v. 20). In Bible times, clothes spoke volumes about who the wearer was and what he or she was experiencing. A king's robes, a beggar's rags, and a mourner's sackcloth all told a story about the ones who wore them. We presume King David removed his mourning clothes and put on his regular kingly attire.

In the Book of Isaiah, the prophet spoke of the Anointed One, the Messiah, Who will comfort all who mourn. He said the Anointed One will console those who mourn in Zion, that He will give them beauty for ashes, the oil of joy for mourning, and the garment of praise for the spirit of heaviness (Isaiah 61:3).

David went to the house of the Lord and worshiped (v. 20). In spite of the pain David may have experienced when his son died, in spite of how bad he may have felt about the situation, he turned to God and honored Him in worship.

David went back to his home (v. 20). Life was going to continue. David went back to his normal surroundings and returned to his regular activities.

David ate (v. 20). Again, life continues, and people need nourishment to live. David said in reference to God, *"You prepare a table before me in the presence of my enemies . . ."* (Psalm 23:5). David understood that life on this earth will not be free from challenges and adversaries, but that God abides with us, meets our needs, and provides sustenance for our lives in the midst of potential threats and dangers.

David put the matter into eternal perspective (vv. 22–23). David's servants were confused. They thought that if he was refusing food and refusing to get up while his child was sick, his condition would certainly deteriorate when he found out that the child had died. To their surprise, upon hearing of his son's death, David did all of the things we've just discussed. Then his servants asked him, *"What is this that you have done? You fasted and wept for the child while he was alive, but when the child died, you arose and ate food"* (2 Samuel 12:21). David expressed his awareness of two realities when he responded, *". . . While the child was alive, I fasted and wept; for I said, 'Who can tell whether the Lord will be gracious to me, that the child may live?' "But now he is dead; why should I fast? Can I bring him back again? I shall go to him, but he shall not return to me"* (2 Samuel 12:22–23).

David recognized the physical, earthly reality: "My son is dead; why should I fast? Can I bring him back again?" David knew it was futile to try to make things the way they were; he could not live in the past. But there was an eternal reality that David also grasped. He said, "I shall go to him, but he shall not return to me." Between the time his son died and the time that he would "go to him," David had to live the rest of his life. This is what adjustment is all about.

Adjustment is going to be different for each person. Every individual has his or her own unique personality and temperament that processes information and perceives events differently. Each grieving person had his own unique relationship with the person who died, and each one will have to make adjustments accordingly.

Please don't read David's account and feel there is something wrong with you if your recovery from the death of a loved one is not as fast and simple as the flipping of a light switch. As we've noted previously, for most people recovery from significant loss is a lengthier process. But be assured that regardless of the time issues you encounter in recovering and adjusting, God is with you every step of the way.

Missing someone you love is a tribute to that person and to his or her influence in your life. Moving forward, making the necessary adjustments, and finding new purpose for yourself is a tribute to God and to His influence in your life.

---

[1] Taken from 101 Hymn Stories © 1982 by Kenneth W. Osbeck. Published by Kregel Publications, Grand Rapids, MI. Used by permission of the publisher. All rights reserved.

[2] Warren W. Wiersbe and Lloyd M. Perry, *The Wycliffe Handbook of Preaching and Preachers* (Chicago: Moody Press, 1984), p. 194.

chapter 7

HOW TO HELP AND NOT HURT:
INSIGHTS ON GIVING AND RECEIVING COMFORT

As the bereaved adjust to their new reality, friends and family will typically reach out in an attempt to lend a helping hand. If you have ever felt the sting of an insensitive remark or the kindness of a gentle word aptly spoken, then you know the power we wield when trying to comfort the grieving. We can either wound with our words or play a vital part in helping to mend the brokenhearted.

During tense and awkward moments, it helps to have a sense of what to say and how to say it. And in moments of great pain or turmoil, we may need help knowing how to receive consolation from others. At various times in life, we all need insight on how to give and receive comfort. The Bible has much to say about helping each other at such times.

ROMANS 12:15
15 Rejoice with those who rejoice, and weep with those who weep.

1 CORINTHIANS 12:26
26 And if one member suffers, all the members suffer with it; or if one member is honored, all the members rejoice with it.

2 CORINTHIANS 1:3–4

3   Blessed be the God and Father of our Lord Jesus Christ, the Father of mercies and God of all comfort,

4   who comforts us in all our tribulation, that we may be able to comfort those who are in any trouble, with the comfort with which we ourselves are comforted by God.

Paul taught that we are not to pull away from people who are in distress, nor are we to avoid people and leave them isolated in their grief. While God has promised to comfort those who mourn, it is important for us to know that He intends to do at least some of that comforting through us. We are the Body of Christ, and we are His representatives on the earth. He desires to express His grace and comfort *through us* as well as *to us*.

CONFRONTING OUR OWN INSECURITIES

Unfortunately, the fact is that many of us are very uncomfortable around people who are grieving. We may feel awkward and not know what to say. One of the fears people have is that of saying the wrong thing. When I was in my early teens, the father of a friend of mine was killed in a car accident. I remember feeling very much at a loss as to what I should do or say. It was easy to keep myself removed from the situation by telling myself, *He probably just needs time with his family and to be by himself.* In hindsight, I believe that most of my reasoning was a way of protecting myself from my own discomfort in being around someone else's grief.

If we are nervous concerning a friend who is grieving, we tend to do one of two things: we either avoid the person altogether, or we become excessively talkative in our nervousness and perhaps begin spouting off all kinds of philosophical or theological clichés.

When a person is dazed, stunned, and reeling from having just learned of the death of a loved one, he is unable to appreciate or comprehend lengthy discourses. Even if intentions are good and the content of the communication is correct, someone who rambles incessantly may come off as annoying and bothersome to the bereaved. However, the calm, reassuring presence of a friend who is sensitive and patient, and who listens and shares briefly, will be appreciated during times of shock and distress.

No one intentionally wants to be an irritant to someone who is already grieving. We want to help, not add more hurt, but how can we be sure to help—both spiritually and practically?

TAKING THE PRESSURE OFF

Perhaps one of the best things we can do to take this pressure off ourselves is to realize that it is not our job to make the person's grief disappear. If we are uneasy with someone's manifestation of emotions or tears, we may scramble to say some kind of "magic words" to make them stop crying and to extinguish their emotional expression. In such cases, what we are really doing is trying to control the situation—and the person—to minimize our own discomfort. But whose needs are we trying to meet at that moment? The fact is that the other person may need to cry or release their emotions at that point. Is it our job to make them stop crying so we won't feel uncomfortable? No, a true comforter is focused on meeting the needs of the other person, not on catering to his own personal comfort.

Grieving people can quickly sense when their grief is being "shut down" by someone who is uncomfortable. When the bereaved sense this, they will often suppress their grief because they are very much aware that the other person is not giving them "permission" to grieve. People in grief often

73

end up feeling totally isolated from others because they don't know when they're going to encounter such disapproval. As a result, they may just get into the habit of putting on a front, because they don't want to run the risk of feeling condemned by their friends.

If we understand that a person who has lost a loved one is going to hurt and go through certain emotions for a season, we can accept that fact, relax, and just be a supportive friend to him or her as he or she works through those emotions over time and makes the necessary adjustments. It is important that we take the pressure off ourselves so that we are not putting negative pressure on the person we are trying to help.

It is not an issue of having a magic wand to make everything instantaneously perfect and pain-free for the bereaved. We can show love, comfort, and support without the pressure of feeling as though we have to provide a quick fix for them.

'THE THING THAT HELPED ME THE MOST . . .'

Let's consider comments from numerous people about the help they received from others following the loss of a loved one.

"When my mother died, our family became totally out of balance in our relationships to each other and in our responsibilities and roles—somebody very important was missing! Twelve years later, somebody who knew about the grief process redeemed me from my silence and helped me to talk, to express myself."

"The thing that helped me the most was a friend just being there for me, dropping everything else and being a shoulder to cry on."

"I was given two bits of great advice that helped me: I was told that everyone grieves in their own unique way and that I

didn't need to conform to someone else's expectations in order to be okay. And I was advised not to make hasty decisions while I was grieving."

"My sister just lets me talk with very little comment, but great empathy."

"My pastor let me know that it wasn't going to be easy, but that I would come through it. It wasn't easy, and I did make it through. My pastor also talked to my husband and let him know that my emotions might change from one minute to the next, and he helped him know how to deal with me during this time."

"No one forced me to put on a happy face and ignore my sadness over my grandmother's death."

"My husband just let me cry and loved on me. He didn't push me to talk about it or to not talk about it."

"A pastor who had lost his wife to cancer told me, 'When you think you're losing your mind, you're not. You'll be okay.' That helped me realize my feelings were normal and would pass."

"The most helpful were those who just listened, and did not say they understood when they had not been through the loss of a loved one."

"The thing that helped the most was when my step-mom began to do a photo album/family history about my mom. Friends of my mom began to share memories about her, things she used to do and say. As much as it hurt at times, I think remembering Mom helped me the most. We didn't make a shrine or anything like that, but we remembered the good times and vowed to make more of our own, because that's what Mom would have wanted."

"When my mother died, my wife stood by me and helped me spiritually and emotionally, even when my nerves were raw. I know I was sometimes difficult for her to deal with.

She validated my feelings with words of kindness directed toward the memory of my mother."

"The most helpful thing a person did was to allow me to go to their kitchen table to just sit, sometimes to talk, and to have coffee. This allowed me a place to go when I couldn't face all the memories surrounding me each day in our house."

"I benefited so much when people opened up 'the topic' for discussion . . . when they acknowledged her death and asked how I was dealing with it or how I was doing, when they asked about her and who she was. The depths of me screamed out to talk about it! Talking about it helped me get through it. To me, it also celebrated her life. She was now a memory, and talking about her helps keep the memory alive. It hurt when people I was close to avoided talking about her death. It seemed that because they didn't know what to say, they just chose to say nothing. I wondered if they were even concerned or cared about her death."

"I found that every word or action, when done in love and from a heart of love, means something. It doesn't matter if you don't know what to say, just say something, do something. It will be a memorial to the person who passed away and an honor to the person who is still here."

"It's important to have loving, caring people around you so that you're not isolated. A hug can mean more than words in a situation like this."

"I am a nurse, and I've taken several psychology courses. I've taken a death and grief course, but when it happens to you, a lot goes right out the window. There is a huge difference between intellectually knowing something as opposed to subjectively experiencing it. You need friends and family, and especially your pastor and church, to help you through the difficult time."

In some cases, what we say isn't as important as how we make the other person feel. Occasionally, people remember very specific words that were spoken to them after the death of a loved one. But more often, people remember how others made them feel long after they have forgotten the words that were said. People can sense sincerity and genuineness. If you conduct yourself in such a way that people who are hurting know you genuinely care, you will make a positive impact in their life that will very likely be remembered and appreciated for years.

WHEN 'HELP' ISN'T HELPFUL

We discussed in a previous chapter the problems of Job's "comforters." They became offended at many of the statements Job made and felt it was necessary to correct him. However, their original actions when they heard of Job's adversity were more in line with true friendship than the way they eventually behaved when the situation turned adversarial.

JOB 2:11–13

11 Now when Job's three friends heard of all this adversity that had come upon him, each one came from his own place—Eliphaz the Temanite, Bildad the Shuhite, and Zophar the Naamathite. For they had made an appointment together to come and mourn with him, and to comfort him.

12 And when they raised their eyes from afar, and did not recognize him, they lifted their voices and wept; and each one tore his robe and sprinkled dust on his head toward heaven.

13 So they sat down with him on the ground seven days and seven nights, and no one spoke a word to him, for they saw that his grief was very great.

Notice how the process started: Job's three friends went to mourn with him and to comfort him. That is biblical and is a true expression of kindness. The first thing they did was to provide companionship and presence. They were just *with* him; they did not try to counsel him or preach to him. They cried on his behalf and sat with him without speaking for seven days and nights. We certainly can't fault their intentions, for it appears to be true friendship that would lead them to simply sit with Job for an entire week!

Once Job began speaking, though, his friends did not sit passively by; they felt compelled to correct what they felt were Job's theological inaccuracies. A young man by the name of Elihu, who observed the argument between Job and his friends, became very angry at Job's three friends *"because they had found no answer, and yet had condemned Job"* (Job 32:3). Job responded bitterly to the condemning approach of those he called "miserable comforters" (Job 16:2) with the following statements:

JOB 13:4–5
4 But you forgers of lies, You are all worthless physicians.
5 Oh, that you would be silent, And it would be your wisdom!

JOB 19:13–14
13 . . . my acquaintances are completely estranged from me.
14 My relatives have failed, And my close friends have forgotten me.

Instead of being helpful, Job's friends actually increased the volatility of the situation, pouring fuel on an already raging fire.

WHEN PEOPLE FAIL US

When we experience a major loss, it would be ideal if everyone responded to our hurts and to us perfectly. We would love it if everyone were sensitive, compassionate, caring, and wise. However, reality is that people aren't perfect. While they typically mean well, people may say or do the wrong thing. Or perhaps they may not say or do a right thing, and the omission leaves us in want of much needed comfort.

"I was a small child when my grandmother died. My mother tried to protect me by not having me attend the funeral or having me around the family while they were grieving. Because I wasn't a part of the group, I ended up feeling excluded."

"It bothered me when people would not talk about it at all. They avoided the issue completely and acted like nothing had happened. There were lots of people before the funeral and at the service, but the day after there was not a soul. Everybody just went back into their busy lives and activities, and I was left to deal with everything alone."

"There were some believers who ridiculed me because I could still laugh. They didn't think I was sad or mournful enough."

"An individual asked if my loved one who had passed away was saved. When I said that I didn't know, this individual told me that I just needed to 'blow it off in order to move on.'"

"It hurt when people presumed to know just how I was feeling, when, in fact, they didn't have a clue as to how I was feeling."

"My pastor's wife told me that grief shouldn't last more than two weeks. Anything more than that was selfish. Though we had gone to them for help, we really didn't get any."

"The most difficult thing I encountered was my family. No one in my family really talked about their emotions or how they were feeling. I felt overlooked in everything."

What do we do when we face disappointment upon disappointment? What do we do when friends and relatives compound the disappointment of losing a loved one by acting in ways that leave us feeling even more hurt? Of course, we need to forgive them, but we can also learn and grow from the experience. We can become wiser and more sensitive to help others in the future.

A MATTER OF PERCEPTIONS AND EXPECTATIONS

Our perceptions and expectations have a lot to do with how we evaluate the kind of comfort and help we receive. I have seen situations where people greatly extended themselves to serve, help, and comfort a person, and yet their efforts were judged by the bereaved to be insufficient. It was obvious that nothing anyone did was going to be enough to satisfy the hurting individual. I have also observed other cases where the grieving person had minimal expectations and regarded even the smallest act of kindness with great appreciation and overwhelming gratitude.

Our judgment can be somewhat impaired, especially when our emotional equilibrium has been shaken by grief. We might have the impression that someone did not do a good job of supporting us or comforting us, when, in fact, his or her efforts may have been quite commendable. We may have unrealistic expectations or be so distressed that anything short of them bringing our loved one back to us and making life the way it used to be is seen as "faulty comforting."

This tendency is important to keep in mind if you are trying to help someone through grief and you sense the person's anger is directed at you. It is very likely that the anger you sense is an expression of what is going on inside the grieving individual, not a reflection of you or your efforts. Do your best not to take the person's anger personally.

BENEFITING EITHER WAY

When people around us truly model Christ's love toward us, we can be deeply touched. We can remember their kindness and endeavor to model that same Christ-like compassion and support to others. However, when people fall short of our expectations or desires, we can still benefit by learning what *not* to do. Instead of developing a martyr complex and perpetually living with a victim mentality because others did not meet our needs, we can draw strength from the One who will never fail us.

The Apostle Paul knew what it was to have people minister to him in his time of need, but he also knew what it was to have people miserably fail "the friend test." While he is not referring to a loved one who died in the following scriptures, Paul is writing about what was still a challenging time of loss for him—he was a prisoner and had lost the freedom to go about as he pleased. He noted people who abandoned him, but he then spoke fondly of someone who had been a true friend. We see both a bad example and a great example of what friendship is all about.

2 TIMOTHY 1:15–18

15 This you know, that all those in Asia have turned away from me, among whom are Phygellus and Hermogenes.

16 The Lord grant mercy to the household of Onesiphorus, for he often refreshed me, and was not ashamed of my chain;

17 but when he arrived in Rome, he sought me out very zealously and found me.

18 The Lord grant to him that he may find mercy from the Lord in that Day—and you know very well how many ways he ministered to me at Ephesus.

The *New Living Translation* renders verse 16, "May the Lord show special kindness to Onesiphorus and all his family because he often visited and encouraged me." The *New International Version* translates the last part of verse 18 as, "You know very well in how many ways he helped me in Ephesus."

A friend like Onesiphorus is truly a gift from God. When facing a difficult time, we greatly value someone who:

- Often visits, encourages, and refreshes us.
- Is not ashamed of our chains (or the problem we are experiencing).
- Very diligently seeks us out and finds us.
- Ministers to and helps us in many ways.

When we are in crisis, it is understandable that we cry out to God, "Lord, send me an Onesiphorus!" As God ministers to us, blesses us, and restores us, our prayer should then become, "Lord, make me an Onesiphorus to someone else."

If someone has been a great comforter to you, you can express gratitude by becoming a comforter to someone else. If you did not have a great (human) comforter when you went through a time of trouble, you can express mercy by becoming to someone else what you would have appreciated but did not have the privilege of experiencing.

THE FRIEND WHO STICKS CLOSER THAN A BROTHER

Having referred to Phygellus and Hermogenes in Second Timothy chapter 1 as men who abandoned him, Paul again refers to people not coming through for him when he needed their support in Second Timothy chapter 4.

2 TIMOTHY 4:16–18

16 At my first defense no one stood with me, but all forsook me. May it not be charged against them.

17 But the Lord stood with me and strengthened me, so that the message might be preached fully through me, and that all the Gentiles might hear. And I was delivered out of the mouth of the lion.

18 And the Lord will deliver me from every evil work and preserve me for His heavenly kingdom. To Him be glory forever and ever. Amen!

Even though people failed Paul, which was no doubt disappointing, he still was able to conclude his comments with a note of triumph. Paul had learned the great secret of trusting in God and drawing from *His* strength, whether or not people did what was right. Regardless of how our human friends treat us in our time of need, we have the comfort of a Friend who sticks closer than a brother (Proverbs 18:24). Jesus will never let us down!

BEING HELPFUL IN PRACTICAL WAYS

It has been said that knowledge is power. This is very true when it comes to having enough confidence to step into a grieving person's life, believing we can make a positive difference. Equipped with knowledge, we can have the courage and confidence to minister to the hurting. Here are some practical steps we can take and insights we can remember in order to offer help that is truly helpful:

- Provide the "ministry of presence."
- Help with organizational matters.
- Help with practical matters.
- Be specific in your offers of assistance.
- Don't feel obligated to preach or be omniscient (all-knowing).
- Touch base regularly.
- Help your friend reintegrate into life's activities.
- Refer when appropriate.

- Don't put unreasonable expectations on your friend.
- Bring up "the topic" and talk about the person who died.
- Remember that children also need help in dealing with grief.
- Recognize that parents who experience a miscarriage or stillbirth also need expressions of love and support.

PROVIDE THE 'MINISTRY OF PRESENCE'

Perhaps the most underestimated ministry in helping people who have lost a loved one is the ministry of presence. By this we simply mean being with someone in a supportive, non-judgmental way as a representative of God's caring presence. While the value of prayer, God's Word, and "speaking the truth in love" is indisputable, we also recognize that the very Scriptures we honor state that there is "a time to keep silence and a time to speak" (Ecclesiastes 3:7). Don't be afraid of silence. It's okay to sit with someone in silence, being respectful and available if and when that person wants to talk.

The fact that a person may seem to be doing well a day or two after the death does not mean he or she wouldn't greatly benefit from the ministry of presence as time progresses. Especially in cases of sudden, unexpected death, it is typically not advisable for the survivor to be left alone at first— someone should stay with them. Again, it is also important that the person who lost a loved one senses that they have "permission" to grieve.

HELP WITH ORGANIZATIONAL MATTERS

A person whose loved one has just died may need assistance in thinking clearly, getting organized, and making plans. Decisions may need to be made regarding organ donation, contacting friends and relatives, meeting with the funeral home, and so on. Depending on your relationship with the bereaved, you may be a great asset in assisting them with these matters (the closer your friendship, the more likely you are to be involved with them). A caregiver can also provide gentle guidance and support as the multitude of details and decisions concerning a memorial service are addressed.

HELP WITH PRACTICAL MATTERS

If the bereaved is not steady following the death of a loved one, it is beneficial if someone can drive them wherever they may need to go. There may be many other areas where practical assistance can be offered: child-care, housecleaning, errands, meals, etc. Of course there is a balance to be maintained. It is advisable not to smother the bereaved or prevent them from doing what they are able to do. Even though they may not be functioning at their highest level, it is typically beneficial for them to do what they can do—even though their functioning and decision-making capabilities may seem impaired. Doing too much long-term or doing things for the bereaved that they should do for themselves communicates to them that you think they are helpless, incompetent, and damaged beyond repair.

BE SPECIFIC IN YOUR OFFERS OF ASSISTANCE

It is better to make specific offers concerning help as opposed to general offers. For example, it is not advisable to say to a person who just learned of a loved one's death, "Just let me know if there's anything I can do to help." The reason this is not the best way to offer help is that the individual's thinking is often cloudy, and the person may not have his or her thoughts organized enough even to know what to ask for.

Further, some people hesitate to ask for something specific because they don't want to impose on others.

It is typically more helpful to offer specific forms of assistance:

- "May I help you with calling friends and family members?"

- "Why don't we sit down together and make a list of what needs to be done?"

- "I'd like to bring dinner over this evening. May I?"

- "Would you like me to pick up incoming family members at the airport?"

- "May I help you with your children over the next few days?"

- "Would you like me to drive you to the funeral home and be with you while you make arrangements?"

Don't be offended if the person declines your offers, and don't be pushy if the person says no. The individual may have others who are also assisting. You have done your part by offering; just remain available for any future assistance you can supply.

DON'T FEEL OBLIGATED TO PREACH OR BE OMNISCIENT

Don't be afraid to say, "I don't know." When your friend asks difficult questions, don't be afraid to not have all the answers. You are not omniscient—only God is all-knowing. In early conversations, don't be afraid to say such things as:

- "I don't know what to say, but I'm sorry about what you're going through. And I just want you to know that I love you, and I'm praying for you."

- "I can only imagine what you're going through, but I really do care for you and want to help you in any way I can."

- "Even though I'm sure that what I'm feeling is only a fraction of what you're feeling right now, I'm hurting with you, and I'm standing with you."

Do what you can do, and as it is appropriate, share what you know to encourage your friend. Know that it's okay for your friend to struggle with certain questions or issues for a while. Certain frustrations and adjustments may take time to work through. Your job is to offer comfort and support, not instant resolutions to all the mysteries of the universe. There are definitely occasions when sharing scriptures or praying with your friend is appropriate, but there will also be times when the greatest gift you can give your friend is that of a listening ear. Remember that people don't care how much you know until they know how much you care.

TOUCH BASE REGULARLY

It's important to realize that a grieving person often receives many expressions of love—flowers, cards, phone calls, casseroles, etc.—for the first few days following the death of a loved one. After that, it's not unusual for everyone else to promptly get back to business as usual and forget about the person's loss. About the time the flowers wither and die, the shock often wears off and a deep sense of pain sets in. When he or she really begins needing support, the phone calls and cards of support have all but stopped coming. A wise friend will be aware of these timing issues and will periodically touch base with the bereaved. Some caregivers find it helpful to mark periodic dates on their calendar just to be sure they consistently stay in touch on this important issue.

It is also important to be aware that holidays, birthdays, and anniversaries can be especially difficult times for people following the death of a loved one. A follow-up call or card just to let the bereaved know you're thinking of them can be very meaningful and uplifting.

HELP YOUR FRIEND REINTEGRATE INTO LIFE'S ACTIVITIES

People who have lost a loved one often have trouble resuming normal activities. For example, if a grieving individual always went to church with his or her spouse, going to church alone may be very painful because it is another reminder that the spouse is no longer present. Perhaps you can help bridge the transition by offering to drive the bereaved to church or sit with him or her during services.

Don't be surprised if you meet some reluctance or resistance in certain areas, and don't be obnoxious in dealing with your friend. Often a loving, gentle persistence is required to help your friend become reintegrated into life's activities. Be respectful of the time factor in this regard as well, and realize that most people will "reactivate" progressively and gradually, as opposed to instantaneously.

REFER WHEN APPROPRIATE

Encourage your friend to seek out and receive whatever level of help is necessary. Perhaps he or she needs to meet with someone who has more expertise than what you have to offer. That does not reflect negatively upon you or your abilities; people have experience, skills, and specialization in different areas. You may have never faced what your friend is going through, or you may have no specific training in how to minister to a person facing what your friend is encountering.

Perhaps your friend would benefit from visiting a pastor or counselor or attending a support group. If your friend is really struggling, you might even offer to go with him or her as a means of moral support. Your friend may also need legal, financial, or medical counsel. Encourage him or her to receive whatever help he or she needs.

DON'T PUT UNREASONABLE EXPECTATIONS ON YOUR FRIEND

You may have faced a loss similar to what your friend is experiencing, but that is no indication that your friend will (or should) go through the experience in the same way you did. You may have an entirely different personality or temperament than your friend, and there may be dozens of other variables that will determine the type of effect this loss has on his or her life. Keep in mind that your friend is a unique individual, and be respectful of that fact.

We must be careful that we are truly sensitive to grieving individuals and are not simply intent on meeting our own needs by superimposing our own story upon that of a grieving person. For example, Mary had just lost her mother. She came across her friend, Sue, and told her about her recent loss. Sue immediately began, "Well, when I lost my mother . . ." and went on and on about her own loss. Sue was more interested in telling her story than she was in taking the time to listen to Mary talk about what Mary was going through.

Instead of Sue assuming that Mary wanted to hear her story, Sue should have listened first and exhibited sensitivity to what Mary needed at that moment. What Sue had to share may have greatly encouraged and benefited Mary, but Mary might have already had an overload of people saying, "That reminds me of the time when I . . ." If Mary withdrew and isolated herself, it may be because she was weary of being bombarded with everyone else's story and felt like no one cared enough to listen to *her*, to hear what she was experiencing.

Mary's greatest need may be to pour out her own heart to a caring and listening friend, not to hear someone else's testimony. Can your testimony encourage someone else? Yes. But it is probably best to listen to the grieving person first. After you've focused on his or her needs, consider asking permission to share your own experience.

For example, Sue could have said, "My heart sure goes out to you as I think about the loss you've experienced. My mother passed away three years ago, and I know what a challenging time that was for me. I would be glad to share with you about some of the things I faced in dealing with my own mother's death, but I would want to do so at a time that is good for you. I'd be happy to talk more with you now, but if you would prefer, I can take you out for lunch or dinner." This kind of approach empowers the grieving person to have an element of control in the situation. Instead of politely tolerating a story she might not be in the best emotional condition to hear, Mary would have felt respected in that she had been given the right to say, "I'm really not able to appreciate what you would share right now."

When the grieving person does ask to hear your experience, it is typically unwise to say to a person, "I know just how you feel." A better approach is to share how God has helped you through a similar situation, and let the person establish his own sense of identification with what you shared (if it actually does relate). It is better to present information and allow the grieving person to decide for himself if it fits his situation. For example, you can say, "I don't know if what I went through or what I felt is identical to what you're experiencing, but when my mother died, it was . . . ; I felt . . . ; I experienced . . ." It is much better for the person himself to come to the conclusion, "Hey, that's exactly how I'm feeling!" than for you to tell him that you know how he feels.

Remember, at certain points in time, the grieving person's need to be heard may be far greater than his need to hear you. You may want to pray, "Lord, when I come across a grieving person, help me to be sensitive to what his or her needs are. Give me the wisdom to know when to listen and when to speak. Help me to focus on truly meeting his or her needs, instead of being intent on saying what I have to say."

Along these same lines, it is also ill-advised to tell people how they should or should not feel. For example, telling a person, "You shouldn't feel angry . . ." doesn't do anything to resolve the anger issues in that person's life. In fact, it only tends to make them feel guilty for feeling that way and could lead them to simply put up a front to avoid being judged by others. We are not created to be the judge of anyone's emotions, and we are more helpful when we affirm and encourage people as they express and work through their feelings.

BRING UP 'THE TOPIC' AND TALK ABOUT THE PERSON WHO DIED

You don't have to force people to talk about their deceased loved one, but people are usually very appreciative to know that someone is thinking about them and hasn't forgotten about their loss. People who have lost a loved one are typically pleased when someone reminisces with them about their loved one. Many miss this opportunity, mistakenly thinking that it's better not to bring up in conversation the person who died. Don't think that every reference to the deceased has to be somber or serious. As a matter of fact, humorous, light-hearted reflections can be very uplifting and heartwarming to those who are grieving.

REMEMBER THAT CHILDREN NEED HELP
IN DEALING WITH GRIEF

Sometimes children are left out and pushed to the side as friends focus their support and attention on adults who are grieving. It is important to provide much reassurance, comfort, and affection to children when someone they love has died. Most of all, children need to be reassured that they are safe and that they will be taken care of. Communication should be age-appropriate, but children need to be addressed honestly and openly concerning what has happened. Do not use figures of speech or euphemisms, such as:

- "Grandmother is sleeping." This can cause the child to become afraid of going to sleep because they fear they, too, may not wake up.

- "We lost her." Children naturally assume if something is lost, you look for it until you find it.

- "Grandpa has gone on a trip." This can confuse the child— and perhaps cause great anxiety—the next time Dad (or another loved one) plans a business trip. Will he not come back either?

In talking with children, take time to make sure they understand as much of what you say as possible. One child was simply told that his mother was in heaven. When he saw his mother's body in the casket at the funeral home, he assumed the funeral home was heaven. Some children are content with a very brief explanation, while other children will have many questions. Be sure to conduct yourself in such a way that the child is comfortable and feels welcome to ask questions and talk about what he or she is thinking and feeling.

Also, be sensitive to things that the child may not say. For example, some children will feel guilty and believe that the person's death was somehow their fault, even though such thinking is totally without foundation. It can be helpful to prevent this type of thinking through reassuring conversations with the child.

PARENTS WHO EXPERIENCE A MISCARRIAGE OR STILLBIRTH ALSO NEED EXPRESSIONS OF LOVE AND SUPPORT

Anything you would do to communicate your compassion in the case of any death—flowers, cards, meals, etc.—are appropriate in instances of miscarriages and stillbirths. Also, it is wise (and kind) to refrain from asking questions that would imply that the death was the fault of the mother. Questions such as "Were you taking good care of yourself?" and "Were you eating right?" are insensitive and inappropriate. Also avoid making statements that tend to minimize the grief felt by the parents:

- "You're still young; you can have more children."
- "At least you never got attached to the baby."
- "Thank God for the children you have."
- "Have another baby; it will help you forget."

These statements seem to devalue or discount the family's distress and sorrow, which are very appropriate feelings to have. We must always consider the feelings of those we are attempting to help, making sure that everything we do and say is indeed helping and not adding hurt upon hurt.

While there is no way to address every possible situation you might encounter in comforting and assisting a person who has experienced the death of a loved one, remember that you have the Holy Spirit, the ultimate Comforter, on the inside of you. As you minister to the grieving, He will give you the grace and wisdom you need to be a blessing. Look to Him, and He will guide you as you express His love to those who are hurting.

Part 2

INSIGHTS FROM THE WORD

chapter 8

THE ORIGIN OF DEATH

*If God is good, and if God is all-powerful,
then why do evil and death exist?*

When someone close to us dies, this type of question generates more than a casual, philosophical pondering. This issue penetrates to the very depth and core of our being. Often, our search for an answer is saturated by an overwhelming sense of anguish, distress, and emotional pain. The good news, though, is that our quest can result in discovering and knowing the truth, and Jesus said the truth would make us free (John 8:32).

The ramifications and repercussions of death are vast and far-reaching, affecting individuals, families, and communities in manifold ways. Death's challenge and influence are felt physically, intellectually, emotionally, spiritually, socially, relationally, and financially. Indeed, they affect every realm of our being.

Questions about death invariably lead people to look to God—to ask questions and form opinions about Him. If we arrive at wrong conclusions, we can feel disenchanted, disillusioned, and hopeless. We can even feel as though God is distant, uncaring, undependable, or even sadistic. This is why it is vital to consider God's perspective on death and to arrive at correct conclusions about the issue of death.

Reading the first few chapters of the Book of Genesis, it becomes clear that death was never a part of God's original purpose or intention for mankind. Death is not a reflection of God's wonderful nature toward us.

AN INTRUDER CALLED DEATH

Everything that God created was good. As a matter of fact, in the first chapter of Genesis, the statement "God saw that it was good" is used seven times in reference to His creation. After creating Adam, God set before him a commandment and warned him, making it perfectly clear that disobedience to that command would result in death.

GENESIS 2:15-17
15 Then the Lord God took the man and put him in the garden of Eden to tend and keep it.
16 And the Lord God commanded the man, saying, "Of every tree of the garden you may freely eat;
17 but of the tree of the knowledge of good and evil you shall not eat, for in the day that you eat of it you shall surely die."

Paul's teaching in the New Testament reflects back to this event, saying, *"Therefore, just as through one man sin entered the world, and death through sin, and thus death spread to all men, because all sinned"* (Romans 5:12). This does not mean that when a person dies it is necessarily because of a specific sin he or she has committed. Rather, we have all been born into a fallen race due to Adam's original transgression.

God not only warned man that sin would result in death, but after man transgressed God's commandment, God loved

THE ORIGIN OF DEATH

Adam and Eve enough to communicate the kinds of negative things the human race would experience from that time on.

GENESIS 3:19,22–23

19 "In the sweat of your face you shall eat bread Till you return to the ground, For out of it you were taken; For dust you are, And to dust you shall return."

22 Then the Lord God said, "Behold, the man has become like one of Us, to know good and evil. And now, lest he put out his hand and take also of the tree of life, and eat, and live forever"—

23 therefore the Lord God sent him out of the garden of Eden to till the ground from which he was taken.

Once sin entered the scene, mankind became subject not only to physical death, but to a wide variety of problems and maladies. Man began to experience guilt, shame, fear, and many other destructive consequences. Life as we see it on this earth is far removed from what God intended and desired for His children. What we see in the world today is a corrupted, compromised, and "broken" version of God's original plan. Violence, plagues, poverty, disease, and death were not part of God's plan for His creation.

What does this mean? Does it mean that God is not in control and the universe is falling apart? No, God is sovereign and He reigns over all. He gave man the choice to obey or disobey. He gave man the opportunity to make a mess of things. However, God reserved the right to clean the mess up and to have the final word.

It is interesting to note that following man's sin, God took specific action to keep man from also partaking of the tree of life. It would appear that God in His mercy did not want man to live forever in a perpetually fallen state. God must have felt it better for sin to go ahead and run its course (Romans 6:23

says the wages of sin is death) and for man to have an entirely new beginning in the resurrection.

THREE TYPES OF DEATH

Genesis 2:17 says, *"But of the tree of the knowledge of good and evil you shall not eat, for in the day that you eat of it you shall surely die."* The literal Hebrew reads, *". . . in dying thou shalt die."* This implies there is more than one type of death. The Bible refers to three different types of death. The term "death" in the Bible does not so much refer to *cessation of existence* as it does to a *separation.*

Spiritual death is the separation of the human spirit from God. Spiritual death does not mean that the person's human spirit is nonexistent or is non-functioning, but rather describes a person who is spiritually separated or alienated from the life of God. When a person receives Jesus as his Savior, he passes from spiritual death into spiritual life. He becomes spiritually united with the Lord. Jesus said, *"Most assuredly, I say to you, he who hears My word and believes in Him who sent Me has everlasting life, and shall not come into judgment, but has passed from death into life"* (John 5:24).

Physical death is the separation of the human spirit from the human body. James 2:26 says that the body without the spirit is dead. Paul referred to the same principle when he said, *". . . to be absent from the body [is] to be present with the Lord"* (2 Corinthians 5:8). Man is more than a physical being; he is also a spiritual being.

Eternal death is eternal separation from God. This is also referred to as the second death (Revelation 20:14; 21:8). The Bible tells us that those who overcome through their faith in Jesus shall not be hurt by the second death, and the second death will have no power over those who are part of the first resurrection (Revelation 2:11; 20:6).

GOD IS THE AUTHOR OF LIFE

The believer needs to understand that God is not the author of death. It would be difficult for a person to trust in or love a God who was deemed to be the originator of something that has brought so much pain and heartache to humanity. Jesus wanted to make sure we understood the difference between God's goodness and Satan's destructive nature. He said, *"The thief does not come except to steal, and to kill, and to destroy. I have come that they may have life, and that they may have it more abundantly"* (John 10:10).

The fact that God is the Author of life, not the author of death, is made even more clear in Hebrews 2:14 and 15, which says, *"Inasmuch then as the children have partaken of flesh and blood, He Himself likewise shared in the same, that through death He might destroy him who had the power of death, that is, the devil, and release those who through fear of death were all their lifetime subject to bondage."*

If death had been God's original and ultimate purpose for man, then Jesus' accomplishments on earth would have been contradictory to the will of God the Father. However, the Scriptures make it clear that Jesus came to carry out and fulfill the will of the Father, not to contradict it (John 6:38; Hebrews 10:9).

Jesus completely disassociated Himself from the author of death. He said, *". . . the ruler of this world is coming, and he has nothing in Me"* (John 14:30). At the tomb of Lazarus, Jesus said, *"I am the resurrection and the life. He who believes in Me, though he may die, he shall live. And whoever lives and believes in Me shall never die . . ."* (John 11:25–26).

Jesus presented Himself as the representative of His Heavenly Father—as One who brought the kind of life that was more powerful than death. Jesus came not to support or enforce the death that overtook humanity in the Garden of

Eden, but to destroy it (1 John 3:8). He came to restore and redeem mankind back into relationship with the God whose gift is eternal life (Romans 6:23).

We can rest assured that God is on our side against death! Through man's disobedience, death intruded upon the human race. But through the grace of God, we have been brought back into union with God. Having received Jesus as our Savior and Lord, we are recipients of His gift of eternal life.

Though death appears to be reigning supreme in the world, we who believe can walk by faith, not by sight (2 Corinthians 5:7). Paul said, *"The last enemy that will be destroyed is death"* (1 Corinthians 15:26). The believer stands confident, knowing that even though death has intruded upon the human race, God will have the final word and life—*eternal life*—will ultimately prevail!

chapter 9

WHAT HAPPENS WHEN WE DIE?

From a human perspective, death is certainly an enemy. In death's wake, loved ones are separated from one another, and we feel the pain and sorrow that follows. However, there is another perspective. From God's viewpoint, death is the means whereby His children come into His tangible and manifested presence in heaven. It has been said that God never sees his children die; He just sees them coming home.

Psalm 116:15 says, *"Precious in the sight of the Lord is the death of His saints."* This verse does not mean that God takes delight in the sorrow and heartache of those left behind. On the contrary, God offers comfort to those who mourn. Jesus Himself is described as a High Priest who sympathizes with human weaknesses (Hebrews 4:15).

AN OUTWARD MAN AND AN INWARD MAN

Why is it, then, that the Lord considers the death of His saints precious? It is precious because while death causes us to be absent from this earth, it facilitates our being present with the Lord (2 Corinthians 5:8). The Bible makes it abundantly clear that when a believer dies, his spirit goes immediately into the presence of God.

To better understand this truth, it helps to know that there is both a physical part and a spiritual part to our existence. In Second Corinthians 4:16, Paul indicated that even though our outward man is perishing, our inward man is being renewed day by day.

In addition to establishing the reality of an inward man (the spiritual nature) and an outward man (the physical body), Paul also taught that when a believer's body dies, the inward man goes to heaven.

2 CORINTHIANS 5:1,6–8

1 For we know that if our earthly house, this tent, is destroyed, we have a building from God, a house not made with hands, eternal in the heavens. . . .

6 So we are always confident, knowing that while we are at home in the body we are absent from the Lord.

7 For we walk by faith, not by sight.

8 We are confident, yes, well pleased rather TO BE ABSENT FROM THE BODY AND TO BE PRESENT WITH THE LORD.

PHILIPPIANS 1:20–26

20 According to my earnest expectation and hope that in nothing I shall be ashamed, but with all boldness, as always, so now also Christ will be magnified in my body, whether by life or by death.

21 For to me, to live is Christ, and to die is gain.

22 But if I live on in the flesh, this will mean fruit from my labor; yet what I shall choose I cannot tell.

23 For I am hard pressed between the two, having a desire TO DEPART AND BE WITH CHRIST, WHICH IS FAR BETTER.

24 Nevertheless to remain in the flesh is more needful for you.

25 And being confident of this, I know that I shall remain and continue with you all for your progress and joy of faith,

26 that your rejoicing for me may be more abundant in Jesus Christ by my coming to you again.

Writing under the inspiration of the Holy Spirit, Paul made his point perfectly clear—to be absent from the body is to be present with the Lord! To depart and be with Christ is far better!

When someone we love dies, we may not feel his or her death is better for *us*. However, it is better for *our loved one*. It is not a trite cliché when we say that a Christian who has died has gone to a better place—it is an absolute reality.

DEPARTURE AND DECEASE

Notice that in Philippians 1:23, Paul said he felt pulled in two different directions. Part of him wanted to stay on earth and continue in ministry, but he was also feeling a strong pull heavenward. Paul did not stay in that position of indecision forever—there came a point in his life when he was totally ready to "go home."

2 TIMOTHY 4:6–7

6 For I am already being poured out as a drink offering, and the time of my DEPARTURE is at hand.

7 I have fought the good fight, I have finished the race, I have kept the faith.

Consider the meaning of the term "departure," which Paul used in verse 6.

The word "departure" is a nautical term referring to a ship getting ready to set sail, casting off her shorelines and putting out into the ocean. Paul's idea of death is not a shipwreck, but a ship ready. The ship was built for the open seas, her true element, and to meet the end for which she was designed, she must "depart," and cast off the lines that bind her to the shore.

A ship is never seen to true advantage unless upon the open sea. There, laden with a rich cargo, with sails set for the breeze, headed on an errand of good will for a foreign port, she is fulfilling the true design of her builder. So was man created for eternity, for the larger life and fellowship beyond his earthly existence. There, and there only, he will fulfill the larger design of his Maker and Redeemer.[1]

Just as Paul referred to his impending "departure," Peter also recognized at a certain point that his life on this earth was coming to an end. Consider his words:

2 PETER 1:13–15

13 Yes, I think it is right, as long as I am in this tent, to stir you up by reminding you,

14 knowing that shortly I must put off my tent, just as our Lord Jesus Christ showed me.

15 Moreover I will be careful to ensure that you always have a reminder of these things after my DECEASE.

Where Paul referred to his *departure*, Peter referred to his *decease*. The Greek word that Peter used in verse 15 is the word "exodos." In the Old Testament, the Book of Exodus tells the story of Israel's departure from the land of Egypt. It is the story of a journey. That is exactly what death is. It is not the cessation of existence; it is a journey to another place.

It is also noteworthy that Peter referred to his body as a tent that he would shortly "put off." For a little while, a tent can be a wonderful home. When a hiker is in the mountains enjoying the wonderful outdoors, a tent can be exactly what he needs when he becomes weary and needs a place to rest and be refreshed.

While tents are wonderful for their intended purpose, a person doesn't expect to live in a tent forever. Before long, a person longs to go home and live in a house, a structure that is much more permanent and sturdy than a tent.

When a Christian leaves his "tent" (his body), where does he go? He goes to heaven—to spend eternity in his Father's house. In John 14:2–3, Jesus said, *"In My Father's house are many mansions; if it were not so, I would have told you. I go to prepare a place for you. And if I go and prepare a place for you, I will come again and receive you to Myself; that where I am, there you may be also."*

According to the words of Jesus, we can be confident that a permanent home awaits us in heaven.

BETTER FOR WHOM?

Paul said that to depart and be with Christ is far better (Philippians 1:23). But we need to ask the question: *Better for whom?* From a human standpoint, we never want to see someone we love depart from us.

The great evangelist Charles Finney experienced immense heartache when his wife died. Consider his words, especially how the Lord graciously redirected his perspective, enabling him to see the situation more from a heavenly vantage point than an earthly one.

. . . as I awoke, the thought of my bereavement flashed over my mind with such power! My wife was gone! I should never hear her speak again, nor see her face! Her children were motherless! What should I do? My brain seemed to reel, as if my mind would swing from its pivot. I rose instantly from my bed, exclaiming, "I shall be deranged if I cannot rest in God!" The Lord soon calmed my mind, for that night; but still, at times, seasons of sorrow would come over me, that were almost overwhelming.

One day I was upon my knees, communing with God upon the subject, and all at once he seemed to say to me, "You loved your wife?" "Yes," I said. "Well, did you love her for her own sake, or for your sake? Did you love her, or yourself? If you loved her for her own sake, why do you sorrow that she is with me? Should not her happiness with me, make you rejoice instead of mourn, if you loved her for her own sake? Did you love her," he seemed to say to me, "for my sake? If you loved her for my sake, surely you would not grieve that she is with me. Why do you think of your loss, and lay so much stress upon that, instead of thinking of her gain? Can you be sorrowful, when she is so joyful and happy? If you loved her for her own sake, would you not rejoice in her joy, and be happy in her happiness?"

I can never describe the feelings that came over me, when I seemed to be thus addressed. It produced an instantaneous change in the whole state of my mind. From that moment, sorrow, on account of my loss, was gone forever. I no longer thought of my wife as dead, but as alive, and in the midst of the glories of heaven. [2]

Years ago one of the American churches produced a film about missionary work in Angola entitled, *I'll Sing, Not Cry.* It was based on the book *African Manhunt* by Monroe Scott, which recounted Christ's victories in the lives of Africans. There was the story of Pastor Ngango, whose beloved wife had died. Great numbers came to the funeral, and they wailed in the customary pagan dirge of despair, until Pastor Ngango stood up by the casket and said, "Stop all this yelling and howling." The mourners stood in shocked silence. "This woman was a child of God. She has gone to her Father. I loved her, but today we are not crying, we are singing."

With that he started to sing, "Praise God," and the Christians joined him. It was not a song of despair or fear or sadness. It was a praise to God, a song of Christ's victory, a hymn of confidence.

Across the centuries comes the theme "I'll sing, not cry." [3]

It is important to realize that this transformation in Finney's perspective and emotions did not happen overnight. The Lord knew the right time and the right way to deal with him and bring him to this place of acceptance.

I remember hearing about a group of Christians from a tribe in Africa who view death from the heavenly perspective. They do not refer to Christians who have died as the *departed* (as we often do, and as Paul correctly did from an earthly perspective). Instead, they refer to them by saying they have *arrived*. They speak of the deceased from the heavenly point of view.

A WIN/WIN PROPOSITION

It is essential to understand that for the Christian, death is not a defeat. The Apostle Paul taught that we belong to the Lord both in life and in death.

ROMANS 14:7–9

7 For none of us lives to himself, and no one dies to himself.

8 For if we live, we live to the Lord; and if we die, we die to the Lord. Therefore, whether we live or die, we are the Lord's.

9 For to this end Christ died and rose and lived again, that He might be Lord of both the dead and the living.

Never think of life and death as a win/lose proposition. Some mistakenly think that if a Christian recovers from an illness, it is a victory, but if he dies, it is a defeat. For the Christian, life and death is a win/win proposition. Remember Paul's words in Philippians 1:21: *"For to me, to live is Christ, and to die is gain."* God wants us to live our life here on earth serving and loving Him. And we can live confidently, knowing that when the time of our departure comes, our wonderful Lord will welcome us home and our homecoming will be precious in His sight. Floyd Faust said:

> Probably no one has given us a clearer picture of what death means to a mature Christian than grand old John Quincy Adams. When that remarkable American was turning four-score years, he was hobbling down the street one day in his favorite city of Boston, leaning heavily on a cane. Suddenly a friend slapped him on the shoulder and said, 'Well, how's John Quincy Adams this morning?'
>
> The old man turned slowly, smiled and said, 'Fine, sir, fine! But this old tenement that John Quincy lives in is not so good. The underpinning is about to fall away. The thatch is all gone off the roof, and the windows are so dim John Quincy can hardly see out anymore. As a matter of fact, it wouldn't surprise me if before the winter's over he had to move out. But as for John Quincy Adams, he never was better . . . never was better!
>
> With this, he started hobbling on down the street, believing without a shadow of a doubt that the real John Quincy Adams was not a body that you could ever enclose in a casket or inter in a grave.[4]

Remember, God never sees His children die. He just sees them coming home. That is why the death of His saints—His children—is precious in His sight.

---

[1] Robert Ervin Hough, *The Christian After Death* (Chicago: Moody, 1947), p. 31.

[2] Charles G. Finney, *An Autobiography* (Old Tappan, N.J.: Fleming H. Revell Company, 1876), p. 382.

[3] James L. Christensen, *Difficult Funeral Services* (Old Tappan, N.J.: Fleming H. Revell Company, Div. of Baker Book House Company, 1985), p. 168.

[4] From *Life, Death, Life* by Floyd Faust. Copyright © 1977 by *The Upper Room*. Used by permission of Upper Room Books.

chapter 10

TACKLING THE TOUGH QUESTIONS

When a loved one dies, we are faced with emotions to handle, decisions to make, duties to attend to, responsibilities to bear, and—often hardest of all—questions to answer.

Nearly every pastor will agree that when he or she deals with family members after a loved one's death, the most frequently asked questions have to do with *Why?* This is especially true when the loved one dies at a young age, when the death is sudden and tragic, or when a person suffers much before dying. One person expressed this struggle by saying, "The most troubling feeling was that of blaming God, or just crying out, 'Why, God, why?'"

Richard Exley shared the following insight:

In my counseling with those who question why humans must suffer, sometimes I simplistically explain that we inhabit a planet which is in rebellion, that we are part of a race living outside God's will, and that one consequence of that rebellion is sickness and death. God doesn't send this plague upon people, nor does He will it. It is simply a natural consequence of humanity's fallen state. Although, as believers, we are a new creation in Christ (2 Corinthians 5:17), we remain a part of this human family—a family that is tainted by sin and death.

As a consequence, we too suffer the inevitable repercussions of that fallen state, even though we may be personally committed to the doing of God's will and the coming of His kingdom.

In truth, the cause of sickness and death is not God, but the hated enemy, sin. Not our personal sin necessarily, not a specific sin—for life and death cannot be reduced to a mathematical equation—but the fact of sin.[1]

When an event impacts us deeply, we search for meaning and understanding. We want to feel safe and secure in life, but troubling circumstances and heartbreaking outcomes can seriously challenge our confidence and our belief system. Left unresolved, these issues can be a stumbling block to our relationship with God.

Religion, per se, has provided answers that are simply not satisfying. Perhaps you have heard one or more of the following statements offered as explanation for the death of your loved one:

- "It was God's will for your loved one to die."
- "God is trying to teach you something."
- "Maybe God has called you to be another Job."
- "This might be your cross to bear; maybe that's why God didn't answer your prayers."
- "God needed your loved one more in heaven, so He just plucked a flower from His earthly garden and planted it in His heavenly garden."

Certain answers from people who claim to have strong faith haven't always been satisfying either, especially when they contain no sense of love or compassion. Some grieving people have been told, "Obviously you [or your loved one] didn't have any faith or this wouldn't have happened." And, "There must have been sin in your life [or your loved one's life], and that's why this occurred." Even if such answers were true in a particular case, they would not be helpful to the person. In fact, they would only serve to compound the problem. The survivor would not only have to deal with the death of his loved one and the loss itself, but he would also have to deal with the guilt and condemnation that had been heaped upon him.

I don't believe that people who are wrestling with questions should just be brushed aside with trite, religious clichés or be treated as second-class Christians and made to feel condemned. I am convinced that believers have a responsibility to pour in the oil and the wine (Luke 10:34)—to minister the comfort of the Holy Spirit to the hurting in a compassionate way. Jesus said the Holy Spirit would be our *Comforter*, not our *condemner*!

There are thousands of good, faith-motivating tapes and books in which spiritual "coaches" encourage us to reach for God's highest and best, and thank God for all of them. But we must not be oblivious to the realistic fact that people have to deal with situations that did not turn out the way they desired. We need to help people recover from past disappointments and heartbreak in such a way that they can regain spiritual and emotional health for the rest of their journey through life. I don't want to see hurting people's wounds become "infected" and in so doing prevent them from running their race.

We must realize that even when it seems we've lost a battle, we can still win the war. If our disappointment from apparently losing a battle causes us to quit, we will miss out on the future blessings and victories God has in store for us. We must remember that God *will* have the final word!

WAYS TO DEAL WITH DISAPPOINTMENT

With all that said, let's look at practical and spiritual ways to deal with the disappointment of situations that did not turn out the way you would have liked. Listen to what David said:

PSALM 35:13–14 (*New International Version*)

13 Yet when they were ill, I put on sackcloth and humbled myself with fasting. When my prayers returned to me unanswered,

14 I went about mourning as though for my friend or brother. I bowed my head in grief as though weeping for my mother.

The agony David expressed in this psalm is something to which many people can relate. Read in context, this passage is about how David felt this type of pain for people who were against him, people who were indeed his enemies. How much more pain can be involved when dealing with what seems to be unanswered prayer concerning a loved one or close friend!

Many people will scramble to offer a "theological excuse" for why something happened or didn't happen contrary to our prayers and desires. But the fact is that such occurrences still hurt, whether or not there is an apparent "reason." Not only is there disappointment, but doubts and accusing thoughts will also come at such times as "the accuser of the brethren" (Revelation 12:10) attempts to bring guilt, shame, and condemnation upon us.

When you consider the emotional pain caused by loss, as well as the fact that there is a spiritual adversary who seeks to devour us (1 Peter 5:8), it's no wonder that people have expressed the following types of thoughts.

"I felt abandoned, and I felt I had failed my daughter. I had always told her that God would make things all right. And now her baby was gone, and I couldn't help her. Her feeling that God had rejected her was the most agonizing pain I've ever felt."

"I had trouble, feeling like I hadn't done enough, said enough, or prayed enough."

"I struggled, thinking that maybe I failed to pray right. Was I such an inept Christian that my husband didn't get healed?"

These are hard issues, but they are issues about which we must make a decision. We know that *"where the Spirit of the Lord is, there is liberty"* (2 Corinthians 3:17) and that the truth of God's Word makes us free (John 8:32). So from where do doubt and harassing, tormenting thoughts come? Immediately following his warning about the devil going about as a roaring lion seeking whom he may devour, Peter wrote, *"Resist him, steadfast in the faith . . ."* (1 Peter 5:9). The decision is yours: Will you succumb to the accuser's harassing and tormenting lies, or will you resist him, holding fast to the truth of God's Word despite the situation?

FOUR MAJOR QUESTIONS

As we hold fast to God's Word, we can find answers to the tough questions, including the four main questions (or spiritual issues) that arise when a person experiences a major loss or disappointment.

1. **Did I do something wrong? (Was there sin in my life?)** This question deals with *guilt*.

2. **Did I not have faith?** This question deals with *doubt*.

3. **Why? Why did this happen?** This question deals with *confusion*.

4. **Can I ever trust God again?** This question deals with *fear*.

Let's examine these questions one by one and find answers that are comforting, satisfying, and liberating.

Usually the first question asked by well-meaning Christians is, "When a person does not get his prayer answered, or when he experiences a problem, does that mean there is sin in his life?" This question deals with the issue of *guilt*.

Some people believe that if something bad happens to someone, it automatically means there was sin in that person's life. This was the premise of Job's friends when they condemned him with their accusations. They concluded (wrongly) that because Job was suffering, he had obviously come under God's judgment because of sin in his life. The fact is that problems can come for any number of reasons. This can be illustrated through the different types of "storms" recorded in the Bible.

THREE TYPES OF STORMS IN SCRIPTURE

1. A Storm That Came Because of Disobedience

In the Book of Jonah, we see a prophet who disobeyed God and ran away from God's clear assignment and direction for his life. A great storm came that affected Jonah's life dramatically.

2. A Storm That Came in the Midst of Perfect Obedience

In Mark 4:35, the disciples were doing exactly what Jesus said (passing over to the other side). Yet they still faced a very violent storm. It did not mean that they were out of the will of God or that there was sin in their life.

3. A Storm That Was Encountered Because of the Disobedience of Others

The Apostle Paul encountered a very violent and extended storm in Acts chapter 27, yet he was following the will of God with every fiber of his being. Paul had even perceived that the journey would be extremely hazardous. He warned his captors of impending danger (Paul was a prisoner at the time), but he could not override the freewill of those who made the decision to set sail (Acts 27:1–12).

It is important to realize that not all storms—problems or trials—people encounter are because of a specific sin they may have committed.

THE MISCONCEPTION OF THE DISCIPLES: 'WHO SINNED?'

The disciples apparently believed that every sickness was the direct result of a specific sin. This is evidenced by a question they asked Jesus.

JOHN 9:1–4

1 Now as Jesus passed by, He saw a man who was blind from birth.

2 And His disciples asked Him, saying, "Rabbi, who sinned, this man or his parents, that he was born blind?"

3 Jesus answered, "Neither this man nor his parents sinned, but that the works of God should be revealed in him.

4 "I must work the works of Him who sent Me while it is day; the night is coming when no one can work."

The disciples presumed so strongly that a specific sin was the cause of this blindness that they asked, "*Who* sinned?" They didn't even bother to ask, "*Did* someone sin?" To the disciples, the fact that someone's sin caused the sickness was a foregone conclusion. While Jesus did not say that the man or his parents had never sinned, He did say there was no specific sin in the man's life or in his parents' lives that had caused his blindness.

There is an interesting side note to this passage of Scripture. Some people have mistakenly thought that Jesus said this man was born blind so *that* Jesus could later heal him and God could receive glory. Consider what Merrill C. Tenney, Dean of the Wheaton College Graduate School, had to say:

> Did His [Jesus'] statement mean that the blindness was inflicted on the man for the express purpose of affording an opportunity for healing him? If so, did it not seemingly imply that God would cause an innocent man to suffer half a lifetime of poverty, misery and scorn that He might later demonstrate divine power? Such a view seems repugnant if we believe in the goodness of God.[2]

Tenney explained that the earliest Greek manuscripts of the New Testament were written with no separation between the letters and without punctuation, and that editors and translators added all punctuation at a later time. Tenney then noted that some had suggested the following translation of the text: "Neither did this man sin, nor his parents. But that the works of God should be made manifest in him, we must work the works of him that sent me, while it is day: the night cometh, when no man can work."

That small punctuation shift makes a big difference in the way the verse reads! Jesus did not say that God caused the man to be born blind so He could later heal him. Actually, Jesus never addressed the "why," but He did let the disciples know that the illness was not due to a sin committed by the man or his parents. Jesus never answered the question as to why the man had been born blind; he simply did the work of His Father by healing the man.

But here is the main point I want to make—Jesus completely repudiated and denounced the idea that this man's illness was directly connected to a specific sin committed by either the man or his parents.

In James chapter 5, James conveys the same truth in talking about anointing the sick with oil and praying the prayer of faith. *"And the prayer of faith will save the sick, and the*

Lord will raise him up. And IF he has committed sins, he will be forgiven" (James 5:15). Notice James said, " . . . IF he has sinned. . . ." In other words, James was saying that perhaps a sin of some kind contributed to the sickness and perhaps it didn't. If every sickness was due to a specific sin the person had committed, James would have said, "And since the person obviously committed a sin. . . ."

I'm not trying to minimize the role sin can play in opening the door to certain kinds of problems. Obviously, Jonah's disobedience got him into a lot of trouble. Other scriptures indicate that sin can cause many problems. The point I am making, however, is that it is unscriptural (as well as unmerciful and insensitive) to automatically assume that any person experiencing difficulties or disappointments is in that unfortunate position because of a specific sin he or she committed. *The Bible does not teach that!*

When people have experienced a disappointing loss, they need to be reassured that God's love for them has not changed. They need to know that He will never leave them or forsake them, and that He is committed to helping them through that challenging time in their life.

'DID I NOT HAVE FAITH?'

Now let's examine the second question commonly asked by well-meaning Christians following a tragedy, death, or unanswered prayer: "Did I not have faith?" This question deals with *doubt*.

Faith and healing are strongly connected throughout the Bible. While healing occurred periodically throughout the Old Testament, healing found its greatest expression through the ministry of the Lord Jesus Christ. Jesus Himself reinforced the idea that healing often occurred in response to the faith of an individual (Matthew 9:22; Mark 10:52; Luke 17:19) or in response to the faith of those around that individual (Matthew 15:28; Mark 2:5).

Healing continued throughout the Book of Acts, and the faith connection is seen in Paul's ministry when he saw that a paralytic "had faith to be healed" (Acts 14:9). In addition to those recorded in the Book of Acts, healings are also recorded as occurring through many of the Early Church fathers and by others for centuries after the Church began.

Individuals such as Augustine and Francis of Assisi witnessed instances of divine healing and miracles during their ministries. In more recent times, Martin Luther, whose name is synonymous with the Protestant Reformation, recorded the dramatic healing of a friend in answer to prayer. George Fox, founder of the Quakers, left documentation of one hundred fifty healings. John Wesley, founder of the Methodist movement, recorded in his diary several healing accounts, including the divinely assisted recovery of his horse!

Today, countless people around the world still testify to being healed in response to prayer and faith. As wonderful as this is, and as thankful as we are for everyone who receives healing from heaven, it can be challenging for a family when their loved one does not receive healing. These unfortunate instances may cause people to question the goodness of God or the validity of their faith.

We see in the Bible people having faith for specific results (such as healing), but it is important to realize that our faith ultimately must be focused on something bigger than results or circumstances. In the final analysis, the focus of our faith must be a Person—God Himself.

It is inconsistent with the Bible's teaching to have faith for a person to be healed but to abandon faith because the individual dies. The Apostle Paul presented a faith that transcended circumstances! When Paul said, "*We walk by faith, not by sight*" (2 Corinthians 5:7), he was not addressing issues such as healing or prosperity. He was talking about death. It takes faith to believe that *"to be absent from the body"* is to be *"present with the Lord"* (2 Corinthians 5:8).

Your faith is not invalidated because your loved one died! It takes faith to continue believing. It takes faith to believe:

- That God created us and loves us.
- That God has forgiven us and brought us into right standing with Himself.
- That our loved one is in heaven.
- That our bodies will be gloriously resurrected, immortal and incorruptible.
- That we will be reunited, and that we will be with the Lord forever.

When healing does occur, it is not the ultimate expression of faith; it is merely a temporary extension of our mortal lives here on this earth. Eventually, everyone dies. Even the people that Jesus healed while He was on the earth eventually died. Even Lazarus, whom Jesus raised from the dead, later died. In light of this, it is vital that we have a faith that transcends this physical life. Ultimate faith believes in God and in His Word regardless of whether temporal circumstances are to our liking.

As Rev. Kenneth Hagin Jr. once said, "Our faith in God shouldn't be grounded on understanding everything that happens to us in life. Genuine faith in God determines to believe God's Word regardless of negative situations." He went on to say, "Your faith needs to be so rooted and grounded in God's Word that regardless of circumstances, you can face setbacks, disappointment, or adversity and declare, 'No matter what happens, I believe God!' That's strong, mature faith."[3]

I can't necessarily tell you why your loved one died, but I can tell you that your faith can transcend unpleasant circumstances and unwanted outcomes. I can tell you that faith in God is important in life and in death. Paul said, *"For if we live, we live to the Lord; and if we die, we die to the Lord. Therefore, whether we live or die, we are the Lord's. For to this end Christ died and rose and lived again, that He might be Lord of both the dead and the living"* (Romans 4:8–9).

'WHY?'

Let's look at a third commonly asked question: "Why?" Or, "Why did this happen?" Again, this question deals mainly with *confusion*. It is a question that has kept philosophers and theologians busy for centuries.

It is normal and natural to ask "Why?" If you find answers that help you, and in some cases you certainly will, that is great. If you gain wisdom that helps you to cope with the loss and to live the rest of your life more productively, that is wonderful. But if you have trouble finding a satisfying answer, I want to encourage you not to get hung up on the *why*. Be prepared to leave the situation in the hands of God, as difficult as that may seem, and to move on with your life.

WHEN THERE DOESN'T SEEM TO BE AN EASY ANSWER

Let me share with you a few scriptures that I believe can be helpful when there are no apparent reasons or satisfactory explanations for a given situation.

DEUTERONOMY 29:29

29 The secret things belong to the Lord our God, but those things which are revealed belong to us and to our children forever, that we may do all the words of this law.

Notice there are two different elements brought out in this scripture. There are *secret things*—these are things we won't necessarily understand, and there are *things that are revealed*—things God has made known to us. To put it simply, in the situations of life there are two different dimensions: the things we *do know* and the things we *don't know*. Each person will have to make the choice as to which of these dimensions will be his or her focus.

In situations that are particularly disturbing, the more you focus on the things you don't know (the why's), the more confused and disturbed you may become. However, the more you focus on the things you do know, even the simple, basic truths of Scripture (*God loves me; God is faithful; There is no condemnation to me because I am in Christ; God will never leave me or forsake me; etc.*), the more peace and comfort you will experience.

Sometimes we have to reach a point where we say, "Lord, I don't seem to be receiving any insight as to why things happened the way they did, so I'm just going to have to leave the situation in your hands. If you choose to show me something, fine. But in the meantime I'm just going to walk in the light of what I do know, and praise you for the good things you have shown me in your Word."

MORE SCRIPTURES TO GUIDE US

As much as we would like to always know every possible detail about every situation, it's all right not to know everything. As a matter of fact, the Bible makes it very clear that we *do not* and *will not* know everything about every situation.

1 CORINTHIANS 13:12

12 For now we see in a mirror, dimly, but then face to face. Now I know in part, but then I shall know just as I also am known.

According to Proverbs 3:5 and 6, there are times when our own understanding of a situation is going to be insufficient. Otherwise, we could always lean on our own understanding.

PROVERBS 3:5–6

5 Trust in the Lord with all your heart, And lean not on your own understanding;

6 In all your ways acknowledge Him, And He shall direct your paths.

The reason we need to always lean upon the Lord is because our understanding is sometimes very limited. If we find ourselves in a position of limited understanding, we are told to trust God in spite of what we don't understand. According to this passage in Proverbs, it appears that our level of trust can exceed our level of understanding.

The Apostle Paul made a similar statement in Philippians chapter 4, saying, *"Be anxious for nothing, but in everything by prayer and supplication, with thanksgiving, let your requests be made known to God; and the peace of God, which surpasses all understanding, will guard your hearts and minds through Christ Jesus"* (vv. 6–7). There is a peace that surpasses our level of understanding. In other words, there may be times when we don't understand a given situation, but we can still experience God's peace in the midst of it.

Notice that Paul used the word "guard" in Philippians 4:6. God's peace will protect our heart and mind against guilt, confusion, and condemnation—especially following a disappointing loss. It's at that difficult time when Satan will try to come against us because we are already hurting and are more vulnerable. God's peace can guard us against any kind of attack.

SOMETIMES WE DO KNOW SOME REASONS

Are there some situations in which a reason, or explanation, may be known? Absolutely! Paul described such a situation.

PHILIPPIANS 2:25–30

25 Yet I considered it necessary to send to you Epaphroditus, my brother, fellow worker, and fellow soldier, but your messenger and the one who ministered to my need;

26 since he was longing for you all, and was distressed because you had heard that he was sick.

27 For indeed he was sick almost unto death; but God had mercy on him, and not only on him but on me also, lest I should have sorrow upon sorrow.

28 Therefore I sent him the more eagerly, that when you see him again you may rejoice, and I may be less sorrowful.

29 Receive him therefore in the Lord with all gladness, and hold such men in esteem;

30 BECAUSE FOR THE WORK OF CHRIST HE CAME CLOSE TO DEATH, NOT REGARDING HIS LIFE, to supply what was lacking in your service toward me.

In the *Wuest* translation of the New Testament, part of verse 30 is translated, " . . . he . . . recklessly exposed his life . . . ." In other words, Epaphroditus overworked himself and didn't take care of his health the way he should have.

Some people mistakenly think that if they understood *why*, all of their problems concerning a loved one's death would be solved. That is not true! If Epaphroditus had died from his illness, Paul would still have missed his friend—*even though he would have understood the reason why he had died.* Regardless of our understanding concerning our loved ones' passing, we will still miss them, and we will still have to work through various emotional adjustments following our loss.

Following the death of a loved one, the real question we must ask is not so much *why*, but *what*.

- *What* do I do now?
- *What* steps must I take to move forward in life?
- *What* does God have to say to comfort me and to guide me through this time?
- *What* is God's plan for the rest of my life?

These kinds of questions are more beneficial and more productive to our recovery and our moving forward than the *why* questions.

'CAN I EVER TRUST GOD AGAIN?'

A fourth question that presents itself in a time of disappointment is, "Can I ever trust God again?" This question deals largely with the issue of *fear*.

When disappointment occurs, a person has a choice to make. He can either exalt the circumstances above the Word, or he can exalt the Word above the circumstances.

A person who chooses to maintain a positive faith in the midst of disappointment could take the following type of position:

I prayed for a person and he died. But, thank God, he knew Jesus, and he is in a far better place. He wouldn't come back here if he could. I don't understand why he didn't receive his healing, but that's all right—I don't have to understand everything. I'm going to trust in the Lord with all my heart and not lean to my own understanding. It's disappointing from a natural standpoint, but I'm looking to the Lord for comfort, but I still believe God's Word. I know that God is still God. I choose not to get bitter or become offended at God over this.

*God is faithful regardless of how this situation turned out,
and I'm going to keep walking with Him.*

In the Old Testament, a prophet by the name of Habakkuk
encountered a situation that was full of disappointment from
a circumstantial standpoint. Consider not only his description
about what was going on, but especially note his response to
the very unpleasant circumstances:

HABAKKUK 3:17–19 *(New Living Translation)*

17 Even though the fig trees have no blossoms, and there
are no grapes on the vine; even though the olive crop fails,
and the fields lie empty and barren; even though the flocks
die in the fields, and the cattle barns are empty,
18 yet I will rejoice in the Lord! I will be joyful in the God of
my salvation.
19 The Sovereign Lord is my strength! He will make me as
surefooted as a deer and bring me safely over the mountains.

Habakkuk was essentially saying, "When everything that
could go wrong has gone wrong, when anything that could
have gone right doesn't, I am still going to praise God and
trust Him. I refuse to let go of God. I know that He will lift
me up and cause me to be victorious in the end!"

"Can I ever trust God again?" That is a question only you
can answer, but I pray you will answer it in the affirmative,
confident that God has your best interests at heart and that
He will strengthen you, comfort you, and help you carry on.

BEING IN THE KNOW MEANS YOU CAN SAY 'NO!'

The Apostle Paul faced a multitude of disappointing experiences in his life. He encountered a large number of challenging circumstances throughout his years serving God, but he

continued to love and serve God. Paul was speaking from a proven heart of faith when he penned Romans 8:35–39.

ROMANS 8:35–39

35 Who shall separate us from the love of Christ? Shall tribulation, or distress, or persecution, or famine, or nakedness, or peril, or sword?

36 As it is written: "For Your sake we are killed all day long; We are accounted as sheep for the slaughter."

37 Yet in all these things we are more than conquerors through Him who loved us.

38 For I am persuaded that neither death nor life, nor angels nor principalities nor powers, nor things present nor things to come,

39 nor height nor depth, nor any other created thing, shall be able to separate us from the love of God which is in Christ Jesus our Lord.

When we are convinced of God's faithfulness and persuaded the way Paul was, we can cling to and depend upon God's love. Hebrews 13:5 guarantees that God will never leave us or forsake us. With such knowledge and assurance, we can say no to everything the devil may try to use to torment us.

- You can say *no* to the condemnation the devil tries to bring! You can hold on to the sense of righteousness that you have been given through the grace of God.

- You can say *no* to the doubt the devil tries to bring! You can hold on to your faith.

- You can say *no* to the confusion the devil tries to bring! You can hold on to your sense of peace.

- You can say *no* to the fear the devil tries to bring! You can hold on to your trust in God.

At times, you may receive answers to your questions; at other times, the answers may not come—as you redirect the focus of your faith and choose to keep your attention on God rather than on questions or circumstances, God's peace will fill your heart and mind. Then no matter what happens, you can hold God's hand and walk with Him as you move forward in life.

---

[1] Copyright 1991 by Richard Exley. From *When You Lose Someone You Love*, pp. 19-20. Copied with permission by Cook Communications Ministries. May not be further reproduced. All rights reserved.

[2] Merrill C. Tenney, *John: The Gospel of Belief* (Grand Rapids, Mich.: William B. Eerdmans Publishing Company, 1948, 1976), p. 154. Used by permission.

[3] Kenneth W. Hagin, *Another Look at Faith* (Tulsa: Faith Library Publications, 1996), p. 116.

chapter 11

FREEDOM FROM THE FEAR OF DEATH

"Looking back, I realize I was afraid most of the time—afraid for my children being without a father, afraid of losing everything and it being my fault, afraid of being alone the rest of my life. The only way to face fear is with more of God and His Word (1 John 4:18). Time proved that He is faithful, and that if I kept His Word before me so I could keep believing Him, I would always come out on top."

"The most troubling emotion that I dealt with was fear. If this could happen to a person I knew to be godly, what or who was to say that I couldn't be next?"

A significant part of what Jesus accomplished for us through His death, burial, and resurrection involved liberating us from the bondage that was connected to the fear of death.

Why are people afraid of death? People sometimes have uncertainty, and there is a fear of the unknown. Some try to comfort themselves by reasoning away the unknown or whatever they are afraid of—including hell. John Lennon of The Beatles sang, "Imagine there's no heaven. It's easy if you try. No hell below us, above us only sky." The problem is that imagining something does not exist does not in any way diminish its reality.

It seems that some people, perhaps because of fear, simply want to avoid thinking about death at all. Perhaps they think if they don't give death any thought, it won't happen. Such thinking may lead them to the same place in which Caesar Borgia found himself when he said, "I have provided in the course of my life for everything except death; and now alas! I am to die entirely unprepared."[1]

A father's little girl was on her deathbed. The little girl, though young, understood what was happening to her and asked what it was like to die. The heartbroken father paused, prayed for a moment, asking God for the answer, and then said, "Honey, do you remember the number of times we've been visiting in the den on the sofa with your mother, and after a time you would fall asleep there in my arms or lying on the sofa, and the next morning you would awaken in your bed?" The little girl said yes, she remembered that. The father said, "That's what it's like for one of God's children to die. You will simply go to sleep here, and when you awaken, you'll be with Jesus. You'll be in His loving arms, not ours. But His arms are longer and stronger and far more loving than ours could ever be."[2]

WHEN FEAR BEGAN

The introduction of fear into the human race coincided with mankind's sin in the Garden of Eden. When Adam and Eve transgressed the commandment of God, they entered into a realm of separation from God. When God called out to Adam, he responded, *"I heard Your voice in the garden, and I was afraid because I was naked; and I hid myself"* (Genesis 3:10).

God, however, was not content to see humanity, His prized creation (see Psalm 8:3–6), separated from Him and suffering the consequences of Satan's rule. God loved us so much that He sent Jesus to be our Savior. What did God's plan accomplish? *"He has delivered us from the power of darkness and conveyed us into the kingdom of the Son of His love"* (Colossians 1:13).

We can see clearly from Scripture that deliverance from fear is a vital part of what God desired to accomplish in our lives.

HEBREWS 2:14–15

14 Inasmuch then as the children have partaken of flesh and blood, He Himself likewise shared in the same, that through death He might destroy him who had the power of death, that is, the devil,

15 and release those who through fear of death were all their lifetime subject to bondage.

REVELATION 1:17–18

17 . . . "Do not be afraid; I am the First and the Last.

18 "I am He who lives, and was dead, and behold, I am alive forevermore. Amen. And I have the keys of Hades and of Death."

JOHN 14:1–3

1 "Let not your heart be troubled; you believe in God, believe also in Me.

2 "In My Father's house are many mansions; if it were not so, I would have told you. I go to prepare a place for you.

3 "And if I go and prepare a place for you, I will come again and receive you to Myself; that where I am, there you may be also."

Paul referred to what life was like for us before we were born again when he said, *"At that time you were without Christ, being aliens from the commonwealth of Israel and strangers from the covenants of promise, having no hope and without God in the world"* (Ephesians 2:12). The good news is, our position in life didn't stay that way. The next verse says, *"But now in Christ Jesus you who once were far off have been brought near by the blood of Christ"* (Ephesians 2:13).

Our peace as believers does not come from imagining there is no hell but in knowing we have forgiveness and acceptance through the blood of Jesus Christ. The assurance the Lord gives is wonderful! Romans 8:16 says, "The Spirit himself testifies with our spirit that we are God's children" (*NIV*). The glorious message of the Gospel is that our sins have been forgiven! We have received the gift of eternal life! We have become the sons of God! We are now accepted in the beloved! We have been sealed by the Holy Spirit! We have a home awaiting us in heaven!

Second Corinthians 1:21 and 22 says, "Now it is God who makes both us and you stand firm in Christ. He anointed us, set his seal of ownership on us, and put his Spirit in our hearts as a deposit, guaranteeing what is to come" (*NIV*). Along the same lines, Paul said, "And you also were included in Christ when you heard the word of truth, the gospel of your salvation. Having believed, you were marked in him with a seal, the promised Holy Spirit, who is a deposit guaranteeing our inheritance until the redemption of those who are God's possession—to the praise of his glory" (Ephesians 1:13–14 *NIV*).

SECURITY BREEDS CONFIDENCE

What a tremendous sense of security is available to the believer! Jesus said, *"And I give them eternal life, and they shall never perish; neither shall anyone snatch them out of My hand. My Father, who has given them to Me, is greater than all; and no one is able to snatch them out of My Father's hand"* (John 10:28–29). When Jesus said, "I will never leave you or forsake you" (Hebrews 13:5), He certainly was mindful of and including the fact that His presence would be with us through physical death and beyond.

> "I now feel so weaned from earth, my affections so much in Heaven, that I can leave you all without regret, yet I do not love you less, but God more."
> —William Wilberforce

With this security ours, we can echo the words of Paul who spoke defiantly against death when he said, *"'O Death, where is your sting? O Hades, where is your victory?' The sting of death is sin, and the strength of sin is the law. But thanks be to God, who gives us the victory through our Lord Jesus Christ"* (1 Corinthians 15:55–57). Jesus has taken the sting out of death—a truth the following story so powerfully illustrates:

A boy and his father were driving down a country road on a beautiful spring afternoon, when a bumblebee flew in the car window. The little boy, who was allergic to bee stings, was petrified. The father quickly reached out, grabbed the bee, squeezed it in his hand, and then released it. The boy grew frantic as it buzzed by him. Once again the father reached out his hand, but this time he pointed to his palm. There stuck in his skin was the stinger of the bee. "Do you see this?" he asked. "You don't need to be afraid anymore. I've taken the sting for you." We do not need to fear death anymore. Christ has died and risen again. He has taken the sting from death.[3]

Paul was not afraid of death because he knew death could not and would not separate him from the love of God. Paul said, *"For I am persuaded that neither death nor life, nor angels nor principalities nor powers, nor things present nor things to come, nor height nor depth, nor any other created thing, shall be able to separate us from the love of God which is in Christ Jesus our Lord"* (Romans 8:38–39). Not only did Paul not fear death, he actually had a confidence, assurance, and anticipation that he was going to heaven.

PHILIPPIANS 1:21–26

21 For to me, to live is Christ, and to die is gain.

22 But if I live on in the flesh, this will mean fruit from my labor; yet what I shall choose I cannot tell.

23 For I am hard pressed between the two, having a desire to depart and be with Christ, which is far better.

24 Nevertheless to remain in the flesh is more needful for you.

25 And being confident of this, I know that I shall remain and continue with you all for your progress and joy of faith,

26 that your rejoicing for me may be more abundant in Jesus Christ by my coming to you again.

Notice in this passage that even though Paul had a great desire to be with the Lord, he was also committed to finishing his race here on earth. He wanted to fulfill the will of God for his life here in this realm before "graduating" to heaven. Later, when Paul realized that his time on earth was coming to an end, he spoke triumphantly and with great anticipation about the reward that awaited him.

2 TIMOTHY 4:6–8

6 For I am already being poured out as a drink offering, and the time of my departure is at hand.

7 I have fought the good fight, I have finished the race, I have kept the faith.

8 Finally, there is laid up for me the crown of righteousness, which the Lord, the righteous Judge, will give to me on that Day, and not to me only but also to all who have loved His appearing.

The Lord will give a crown of righteousness *"to all who have loved His appearing"* (v. 8). Jesus has conquered death! We as Christians need not fear it. Our future is not one that involves separation from God or misery—we will simply be going over to our Father's house.

If you happen to experience some fear, does that mean you are not a child of God? Certainly not. But you can overcome fear!

OVERCOMING FEAR AND THE GUILT OF BEING AFRAID

Some believers have heard enough teaching on the subject of fear to know that they are not supposed to be afraid. Consequently, whenever they experience fear they feel ashamed and are hesitant to admit they are having a problem with it. As a result, they become isolated with their fear and the problem becomes worse.

Sometimes it helps us to realize we're not the first to experience any given problem (see 1 Corinthians 10:13). We can draw strength from knowing that God does not turn His back on us when we experience a problem with fear, and we can benefit from seeing that other godly people—even individuals in the Bible—encountered the same problems, looked to God, and were helped. Consider David's words:

PSALM 18:1–6

1 I will love You, O Lord, my strength.

2 The Lord is my rock and my fortress and my deliverer; My God, my strength, in whom I will trust; My shield and the horn of my salvation, my stronghold.

3 I will call upon the Lord, who is worthy to be praised; So shall I be saved from my enemies.

4 The pangs of death surrounded me, And the floods of ungodliness made me afraid.

5 The sorrows of Sheol surrounded me; The snares of death confronted me.

6 In my distress I called upon the Lord, And cried out to my God; He heard my voice from His temple, And my cry came before Him, even to His ears.

Notice that David did not deny the reality of the fear, sorrows, and distress that he experienced. But in spite of these things, he called out to God, and God definitely helped him. Remember that God's love for us is not based upon our perfection. If God waited until we were perfect before He loved or helped us, we would all be in big trouble. God, in His mercy and grace, loves us in spite of our problems, and it is His mercy and grace that help us through and beyond our difficulties.

PSALM 56:3–4,10–11

3 Whenever I am afraid, I will trust in You.

4 In God (I will praise His word), In God I have put my trust; I will not fear. What can flesh do to me?

10 In God (I will praise His word), In the Lord (I will praise His word),

11 In God I have put my trust; I will not be afraid. What can man do to me?

David takes an interesting approach in Psalm 56. At first read, this psalm can seem contradictory. At first David says, "Whenever I am afraid," and then quickly makes the statements, "I will not fear" and "I will not be afraid." It is as though David acknowledges his humanity and his imperfection one moment, but then proclaims his decision and his goal in the next breath. Is that a contradiction? I don't think so. Is it wrong to strive for the highest while being honest about your current condition? No, it is not.

The Apostle Paul was certainly a man who had learned how to trust God through many great dangers, and yet he was honest about what he was going through. He did not put up a false front so people would think he never experienced difficulties or challenges. Consider Paul's very transparent and honest disclosure to the believers in Corinth: *"For we do not want you to be ignorant, brethren, of our trouble which came to us in Asia: that we were burdened beyond measure, above strength, so that we despaired even of life"* (2 Corinthians 1:8).

Could the Apostle Paul despair to the point that he thought he might die? That doesn't sound like a very positive statement! Isn't this the same person who said (even in the same letter) *"Now thanks be to God who always leads us in triumph in Christ"*(2 Corinthians 2:14)? How could Paul, a true Christian, feel such despair—an emotion that contradicts the sense of triumph he described? And yet Paul did, and he was honest about it.

Actually, later in the same epistle to this church Paul was even more graphic about the negative feelings he experienced. Second Corinthians 7:5 says, *"For indeed, when we came to Macedonia, our bodies had no rest, but we were troubled on every side. Outside were conflicts, inside were fears."* Can you imagine the great Apostle acknowledging that he was actually afraid? Of course! Paul wasn't a robot. He wasn't a machine. He was a human being, and like the rest of us, he faced challenges. We can thank God that Paul didn't just share with us the difficulty that he encountered, but he also shared with us how God helped him win the victory. After acknowledging his fear, Paul said in the very next verse, *"Nevertheless God, who comforts the downcast, comforted us by the coming of Titus"* (2 Corinthians 7:6).

LUKE 2:25–32
25 And behold, there was a man in Jerusalem whose name was Simeon, and this man was just and devout, waiting for the Consolation of Israel, and the Holy Spirit was upon him.
26 And it had been revealed to him by the Holy Spirit that he would not see death before he had seen the Lord's Christ.
27 So he came by the Spirit into the temple. And when the parents brought in the Child Jesus, to do for Him according to the custom of the law,
28 he took Him up in his arms and blessed God and said:
29 "Lord, now You are letting Your servant depart in peace, According to Your word;
30 For my eyes have seen Your salvation
31 Which You have prepared before the face of all peoples,
32 A light to bring revelation to the Gentiles, And the glory of Your people Israel."

I find it very interesting that God's comfort for Paul in this particular situation did not come from an audible heavenly voice, from a vision, or from an angelic appearance; it came through a friend. Paul was a human being growing in his walk with God, just as we all are. God did not reject Paul or turn His back on him because he struggled with fear, and God won't reject us either. God helped Paul, and He will help us too.

FAITH IN THE FACE OF DEATH

When it comes to facing death, some people have acknowledged being somewhat unsettled. Yet they were thankful to learn that God's grace was still very real when they needed His help—in spite of their apprehension. When Daniel Webster realized that his time on earth was nearing an end, he wrote the words he wanted on his tombstone: "Lord, I believe; help Thou my unbelief."[4] With this statement, Webster identified with the man who came to Jesus and uttered those same words (see Mark 9:24). In the biblical account, the man acknowledged that his faith wasn't perfect and that he was struggling with unbelief, but he looked to Jesus for help nonetheless. Jesus graciously and mercifully accommodated the man's request.

Question and Answer #1
from The Heidelberg Catechism

Question: What is thy only comfort in life and death?
Answer: That I with body and soul, both in life and death, am not my own, but belong unto my faithful Saviour Jesus Christ; who, with his precious blood, has fully satisfied for all my sins, and delivered me from all the power of the devil; and so preserves me that without the will of my heavenly Father, not a hair can fall from my head; yea, that all things must be subservient to my salvation, and therefore, by his Holy Spirit, He also assures me of eternal life, and makes me sincerely willing and ready, henceforth, to live unto him.

Indicating an initial lack of confidence regarding a peaceful death, Edward Turner, a professor of chemistry at the University of London in the 1800s and a believer in Jesus, said on his deathbed, "I could not have believed that I could be happy on my deathbed. I am content my career to close."[5] Another godly person on his deathbed said, "Ah! is this dying? How have I dreaded as an enemy this smiling friend!"[6] In other words, this individual did not expect death to be a positive experience; nonetheless, God was present, providing grace and comfort.

These two accounts remind me of what Paul said in Second Timothy 2:13: "If we are faithless [do not believe and are untrue to Him], He remains true (faithful to His Word and His righteous character), for He cannot deny Himself" (AMP). We can be very thankful that God's faithfulness is not dependent upon ours. We can also be grateful that even if we experience fear about something, God still loves us and wants to help us overcome every kind of dread and torment.

CONFIDENT CHRISTIANS' LAST WORDS

It is tremendously encouraging to see the hope, confidence, and even enthusiasm with which many Christians have faced death through the years. Don't be discouraged if your faith is still growing toward the types of expressions that follow; *just keep growing*!

- About the year 125 A.D., a Greek by the name of Aristeides was writing to one of his friends about the new religion Christianity. He was trying to explain the reasons for its extraordinary success. Here is a sentence from one of his letters: "If any righteous man among the Christians passes from this world, they rejoice and offer thanks to God, and they escort his body with songs and thanksgiving as if he were setting out from one place to another nearby."[7]

- When that great Christian and scientist, Sir Michael Faraday, was dying, some journalists questioned him as to his speculations for a life after death. "Speculations!" said he, "I know nothing about speculations. I'm resting on certainties. 'I know that my redeemer liveth,' and because He lives, I shall live also."[8]

- "Richard Baxter, author of *The Saints' Everlasting Rest*, faithful among the faithful, and most diligent of pastors, as his frame weakened during his last illness, whispered in response to an inquiry as to how he felt, 'I am almost well.' For Heaven will be the saints' everlasting rest indeed!"[9]

- Realizing that he would soon be gone from this world one day, [Dwight L.] Moody said to a friend, "Someday you will read in the papers that D. L. Moody of Northfield is dead. Don't you believe a word of it. At that moment I shall be more alive than I am now. I shall have gone higher, that is all—out of this old clay tenement into a house that is immortal, a body that sin cannot touch, that sin cannot taint, a body fashioned into His glorious body. I was born in the flesh in 1837; I was born of the Spirit in 1856. That which is born of the flesh may die; that which is born of the Spirit will live forever."[10]

A few hours before entering the "Homeland" Dwight L. Moody caught a glimpse of the glory awaiting him. Awakening from a sleep, he said, "Earth recedes, Heaven opens before me. If this is death, it is sweet! There is no valley here. God is calling me, and I must go." His son who was standing by his bedside said, "No, no father, you are dreaming." "No," said Mr. Moody, "I am not dreaming: I have been within the gates: I have seen the children's faces." A short time elapsed and then, following what seemed to the family to be the death struggle he spoke again: "This is my triumph; this my coronation day! It is glorious!"[11]

- Michelangelo, the Italian artist and sculptor, wrote in his will, "I die in the faith of Jesus Christ and in the firm hope of a better life." On his deathbed, he spoke to those with him and said, "Through life remember the sufferings of Jesus."[12]

Consider also the "last words" of these children of God as they prepared to step into eternity:

"Our God is the God of whom cometh salvation. God is the Lord by whom we escape death."[13]
—Martin Luther

"Live in Christ, live in Christ, and the flesh need not fear death."[14]
—John Knox

"The best of all is, God is with us. . . . Fare-well!"[15]
—John Wesley

". . . I cannot express the thousandth part of what praise is due to Thee. It is but little I can give Thee, but Lord, help me to give Thee my all. I will die praising Thee, and rejoice that others can praise Thee better. I shall be satisfied with Thy likeness! satisfied! satisfied! O my dearest Jesus, I come."[16]
—Charles Wesley

"All is well, and the seed of God reigns over all, and over death itself."[17]
—George Fox

"I rejoice in hope, I am accepted—accepted!"[18]
—John Kent

"A life spent in the service of God and communion with Him is the most comfortable and pleasant life that one can live in this present world."[19]
—Matthew Henry

"Dying is sweet work! sweet work! My heavenly Father, I am looking up to my dear Jesus, my God, my portion, my all in all. Glory, Glory, Home, Home!"[20]
—Samuel Medley

"Only repeat to me the name of Jesus. Whenever I hear it or pronounce it myself I feel refreshed with fresh joy. God be praised, only one hour more."[21]

—Christian F. Gellert

"I shall see Jesus, and that will be grand. I shall see Him who made the worlds."[22]

—David Brewster

"Going out into life—that is dying."[23]

—Henry Ward Beecher

"This is the end of earth, I am content."[24]

—John Quincy Adams

". . . I throw myself on the mercy of God through the merits of Christ."[25]

—William Pitt

"The waters are rising, but so am I. I am not going under but over. Don't be concerned about dying; go on living well, the dying will be right."[26]

—Catherine Booth

"My heart is resting sweetly with Jesus, and my hand is in His."[27]

—Howard Crosby

"I am going where all tears will be wiped away."[28]

—Matthew Cotton

"He will come; and will not tarry. I shall soon be in glory; soon be with God and His angels."[29]

—David Brainerd

"I shall soon be with Him. Victory, Victory, Victory (then raising his hand) for *ever*."[30]

—William Gadsby

"Far from a world of grief and sin, With God eternally shut in. . . . God is faithful! God is faithful."[31]

—John Kershaw

"I know I am dying, but my death-bed is a bed of roses. I have no thorns planted upon my dying pillow. Heaven is already begun!"[32]

—John Pawson

"He has indeed been a precious Christ to me, and now I feel him to be my rock, my strength, my rest, my hope, my joy, my all in all."[33]

—Thomas Rutherford

"It is a great mercy to me that I have no manner of fear or dread of death."[34]

—Isaac Watts

These words express the hope, confidence, and assurance that every believer can have. Because of the love God has for us, we can have boldness on the Day of Judgment. And we can live this earthly life free of fear and torment because God's perfect love casts out fear.

1 JOHN 4:15–19

15 Whoever confesses that Jesus is the Son of God, God abides in him, and he in God.

16 And we have known and believed the love that God has for us. God is love, and he who abides in love abides in God, and God in him.

17 Love has been perfected among us in this: that we may have boldness in the day of judgment; because as He is, so are we in this world.

18 There is no fear in love; but perfect love casts out fear, because fear involves torment. But he who fears has not been made perfect in love.

19 We love Him because He first loved us.

REVELATION 14:13

13 Then I heard a voice from heaven saying to me, "Write: 'Blessed are the dead who die in the Lord from now on.'" "Yes," says the Spirit, "that they may rest from their labors, and their works follow them."

According to Revelation 14:13, blessed are those who die in the Lord—we will rest from our earthly toil and enjoy the glory of heaven that awaits us. In the meantime, we can live in fearless confidence, knowing that when we leave our body we will be present with the Lord! Because of the salvation Jesus wrought in His death, burial, and resurrection, we have been set free from the fear of death!

---

1 Billy Graham, *World Aflame* (Garden City, N.Y.: Doubleday & Company, Inc., 1965), p. 75.

2 Reprinted by permission of Thomas Nelson Publishers from the book entitled *Confessions of a Grieving Christian*, copyright 1998 by Zig Ziglar Corporation.

3 Adrian Dieleman, *Leadership*, Vol. XV, No. 1 (Winter 1994), p. 47.

4 Taken from *Last Words of Saints and Sinners* by Herbert Lockyer © 1969 by Kregel Publications, Grand Rapids, Mich., p. 92. Used by permission of the publisher. All rights reserved.

5 Lockyer, p. 125.

6 Taken from *Encyclopedia of 7,700 Illustrations* by Paul Lee Tan © Bible Communications, Inc. [www.tanbible.com] (Chicago: Assurance Publishers, 1979), p. 314.

7 Tan, p. 309.

8 Tan, p. 311.

9 J.B. Watson, "What Heaven Means to Me," *Heaven—The Home of the Redeemed*, ed. Hy. Pickering (London: Pickering & Inglis), p. 23.

10 Tan, p. 309.

11 Tan, p. 313.

12 Lockyer, p. 125.

13 Lockyer, p. 73.

14 Tan, p. 314.

15 Lockyer, p. 64.

16 Lockyer, p. 120.

[17] Lockyer, p. 55.

[18] Lockyer, p. 121.

[19] *Baker's Funeral Handbook*, ed. Paul E. Engle (Grand Rapids, Mich.: Baker Books, 1996), p. 167.

[20] Lockyer, p. 121.

[21] Lockyer, p. 106.

[22] Lockyer, p. 122.

[23] Lockyer, p. 53.

[24] Lockyer, p. 99.

[25] Lockyer, p. 91.

[26] Lockyer, p. 53.

[27] Lockyer, p. 58.

[28] Lockyer, p. 58.

[29] Lockyer, pp. 63–64.

[30] Lockyer, p. 67.

[31] Lockyer, p. 67.

[32] Tan, p. 314.

[33] *Baker's Funeral Handbook*, p. 168.

[34] *Baker's Funeral Handbook*, p. 168.

chapter 12

HEAVEN:
THE BELIEVER'S HOPE

Here in this world, He bids us come;
There in the next, He shall bid us welcome.
—John Donne

We are more apt to live free from the fear of death when we recognize and understand death for what it truly is. The Bible portrays physical death as more of a transition than a termination. There is an element of termination in the sense that the physical body ceases functioning, but as we read in chapter 9, the Bible describes man as more than just a body, or outward man; the Bible also describes an inward man.

Man is a spiritual being, yet man resides in a body. When the body stops functioning, the spirit of man simply transitions to a new location. For a Christian, that new location is a wonderful place called heaven. Heaven is not a dream. It is not a figment of someone's imagination. Heaven is not a metaphysical abstraction or a theological conception. Jesus did not say, "Our Father which art in a state of mind. . . ." He said, "Our Father which art in heaven . . ." (Matthew 6:9). Heaven is a real place!

Can we even begin to describe heaven? Should we even try? Certainly we are very aware of our immense limitations in such a venture. Jonathan Edwards, the renowned preacher of the Great Awakening in the early days of this country, said, "To pretend to describe the excellence, the greatness or duration of the happiness of heaven by the most artful composition of words would be but to darken and cloud it; to talk of raptures and ecstasies, joy and singing, is but to set forth very low shadows of the reality."[1]

Charles Spurgeon echoed the same sentiments: "When a mortal man speaks anything of that eternal blessedness of the saints in glory, he is like a blind man discoursing about the light which he has never seen, and so cannot distinctly speak anything concerning it." Spurgeon also said, "In a way it is akin to a man writing a travel guide for a land he has never visited or seen. It is to attempt to describe the indescribable with words which cannot come close to expressing the glory of heaven."

Even the Apostle Paul expressed our limitations in knowing all that lies beyond this realm when he said, *"For we know in part and we prophesy in part . . . . For now we see in a mirror, dimly, but then face to face. Now I know in part, but then I shall know just as I also am known"* (1 Corinthians 13:9–12). Paul also indicated the "mystery" aspect of heaven when he referred to an outstanding event he had experienced:

2 CORINTHIANS 12:2–4 (*New Living Translation*)

2 I was caught up into the third heaven fourteen years ago.

3 Whether my body was there or just my spirit, I don't know; only God knows.

4 But I do know that I was caught up into paradise and heard things so astounding that they cannot be told.

The *New King James Version* refers to Paul having heard "inexpressible words," while *The Amplified Bible* uses the phrase "utterances beyond the power of man to put into words."

Admittedly, there are many things about heaven which God has chosen not to reveal to us at this point, but neither has He been entirely silent about what awaits us. We may not be able to grasp or perceive everything there is to know about heaven, but certainly we should be diligent and desirous to know all that we possibly can know about our future home!

HOW MUCH EMPHASIS SHOULD WE PLACE ON HEAVEN?

Many say that Christianity should focus on the here-and-now, helping people to deal with the practicalities and realities of life in this world. However, some take this position to the extreme, speaking disparagingly of any emphasis on heaven. While a large part of the teaching in the New Testament does, in fact, deal with the here-and-now, the Bible also addresses matters of eternity, including life after death and heaven.

When the Holy Spirit inspired the writing of the Scriptures, He gave us an abundance of instruction on how to live successfully in this life, how to relate to others, and how to obey and please God in the practical matters of living. But the Bible does not present our temporal existence and eternal destiny as contradictory issues. They are not in opposition to one another.

The believer does not have to choose between being informed about this life and being inspired about the life hereafter. It is not an either/or proposition—the Bible addresses both issues substantively. For example, the Apostle Paul mentioned that physical exercise can benefit us in this life, but he went on to say that *"bodily exercise profits a little, but*

151

godliness is profitable for all things, having promise of the life that now is and of that which is to come" (1 Timothy 4:8).

It has been said that some Christians are so heavenly minded they're no earthly good. But perhaps more believers are so earthly minded they're no heavenly good. Is it possible that the reason so many people have uncertainty and fear about death is because so little has been taught about heaven?

Granted, we must live and function in this world while we are here. The anticipation of heaven was never meant to be a cop-out from living responsibly on this earth. As believers, we are not to have an "escapist mentality," using heaven as a means of excusing ourselves from fulfilling the plan of God for our lives on earth.

In Luke chapter 19, Jesus told a parable that stresses the need for us to be diligent and faithful stewards here on earth. Luke 19:13 says, "And he called his ten servants, and delivered them ten pounds, and said unto them, Occupy till I come" *(KJV)*. The *New King James Version* renders "occupy till I come" as, *"Do business till I come."* That is what believers are called to do. We are to embrace God's plan for our time here on earth, living life to its fullest.

JUST PASSING THROUGH

Although we are to live life to its fullest, our heart, hopes, and desires can never be ultimately fulfilled here on earth. The Apostle John recognized this and exhorted believers to be mindful that this world is fatally flawed and incapable of providing ultimate satisfaction to the believer.

1 JOHN 2:15–17

15 Do not love the world or the things in the world. If anyone loves the world, the love of the Father is not in him.

16 For all that is in the world—the lust of the flesh, the lust of the eyes, and the pride of life—is not of the Father but is of the world.

17 And the world is passing away, and the lust of it; but he who does the will of God abides forever.

Wise is the person who recognizes the difference between settling down and passing through. The great men and women of God described in Hebrews chapter 11 (what has been called The Hall of Faith) *"confessed that they were strangers and pilgrims on the earth"* (Hebrews 11:13). Peter instructed believers to "live in reverent fear of him during your time as foreigners here on earth" (1 Peter 1:17 *NLT*). First Peter 1:17 in the *Revised Standard Version* refers to the Christian's life here on earth as "the time of your exile." The *Amplified Bible* uses the phrase, "the time of your temporary residence [on the earth, whether long or short]." Jesus said that we are in the world, but not of the world (John 17:11,14).

Expressing similar sentiment, C.S. Lewis said: "Has this world been so kind to you that you should leave with regret? There are better things ahead than any we leave behind."[2] Lewis also said, "If I find in myself a desire which no experience in this world can satisfy, the most probable explanation is that I was made for another world."[3]

Even though our existence here on earth is temporary, God still gave us a wealth of knowledge and information on how to deal successfully in life. In Joshua 1:8, God told Joshua, "This Book of the Law shall not depart out of your mouth, but you shall meditate on it day and night, that you may observe and do according to all that is written in it. For then you shall make your way prosperous, and then you shall deal wisely and have good success" (*AMP*).

God has provided us wonderful wisdom and instruction so that we can deal wisely and have success in the affairs of life. However, from the vantage point of eternity, our life on this earth remains *"a vapor that appears for a little time and then vanishes away"* (James 4:14). If you remove eternity and heaven from the equation, what God has said about the here-and-now becomes ultimately meaningless.

The Apostle Paul lived a life filled with enormous sacrifice for the Gospel. He suffered much persecution because of his commitment to preach God's Word. He paid such a dear price that nothing this world had to offer was worth his efforts. However, the hope of heaven governed Paul, stabilized him, and gave him a supernatural endurance. Paul made it clear that if there was no life after this earthly existence, his attitude and approach to life would have been much different!

1 CORINTHIANS 15:19 (*King James Version*)
19 If in this life only we have hope in Christ, we are of all men most miserable.

1 CORINTHIANS 15:32 (*New Living Translation*)
32 And what value was there in fighting wild beasts—those men of Ephesus—if there will be no resurrection from the dead? If there is no resurrection, "Let's feast and get drunk, for tomorrow we die!"

Paul suffered much and endured much, and yet he also knew great joys in life. But no matter how wonderful God's blessings are in this life, they are a mere shadow compared to the glory, wonder, and indescribable greatness of heaven's majesty. It is unfortunate that some have become so narrowly and exclusively focused on this life that they have failed to develop an eager anticipation of heaven.

LOVING LIFE—DESIRING HEAVEN

Samuel Rutherford once said, "If contentment were here, heaven would not be heaven. I wonder why a child of God would ever have a sad heart, considering what his Lord is preparing for him."

Paul exemplified the connectedness between this life and the next when he said, *"I have fought the good fight, I have finished the race, I have kept the faith"* (2 Timothy 4:7). Paul lived out God's full purpose for his life on earth. Then, just as he had lived his earthly life with zeal and determination, Paul set his sights on heaven with enthusiastic expectation. The very next verse reads, *"Finally, there is laid up for me the crown of righteousness, which the Lord, the righteous Judge, will give to me on that Day, and not to me only but also to all who have loved His appearing"* (2 Timothy 4:8).

People of faith possessing an eager anticipation of heaven are found in many other places throughout Scripture.

PSALM 16:11 *(New Living Translation)*
11 You will show me the way of life, granting me the joy of your presence and the pleasures of living with you forever.

PSALM 73:24
24 You will guide me with Your counsel, And afterward receive me to glory.

LUKE 10:20
20 ". . . rejoice because your names are written in heaven."

ROMANS 8:23 *(New Living Translation)*
23 And even we Christians, although we have the Holy Spirit within us as a foretaste of future glory, also groan to be released from pain and suffering. We, too, wait anxiously for that day when God will give us our full rights as his children, including the new bodies he has promised us.

1 CORINTHIANS 1:7
7 . . . eagerly waiting for the revelation of our Lord Jesus Christ.

2 CORINTHIANS 5:2,8 (*Amplified*)

2   Here indeed, in this [present abode, body], we sigh and groan inwardly, because we yearn to be clothed over [we yearn to put on our celestial body like a garment, to be fitted out] with our heavenly dwelling. . . .

8   [Yes] we have confident and hopeful courage and are pleased rather to be away from home out of the body and be at home with the Lord.

PHILIPPIANS 3:20

20 For our citizenship is in heaven, from which we also eagerly wait for the Savior, the Lord Jesus Christ.

COLOSSIANS 1:5

5   because of the hope which is laid up for you in heaven, of which you heard before in the word of the truth of the gospel.

TITUS 2:13

13 looking for the blessed hope and glorious appearing of our great God and Savior Jesus Christ.

HEBREWS 10:34

34 for you . . . joyfully accepted the plundering of your goods, knowing that you have a better and an enduring possession for yourselves in heaven.

HEBREWS 11:10 (*New Living Translation*)

10 Abraham . . . was confidently looking forward to a city with eternal foundations, a city designed and built by God.

HEBREWS 11:14,16

14 For . . . they seek a homeland. . . .

16 . . . they desire a better, that is, a heavenly country. Therefore God is not ashamed to be called their God, for He has prepared a city for them.

HEBREWS 13:14

14 For here we have no continuing city, but we seek the one to come.

2 PETER 3:13

13 Nevertheless we, according to His promise, look for new heavens and a new earth in which righteousness dwells.

We can follow these biblical examples, and while living a godly life on earth, we can look forward to our life with God in heaven.

IS HEAVEN ON OUR MIND?

Why should the Christian be mindful of heaven? Our living with God in heaven has been on God's mind for a long time.

COLOSSIANS 3:1–4 (*New Living Translation*)

1 Since you have been raised to new life with Christ, set your sights on the realities of heaven, where Christ sits at God's right hand in the place of honor and power.

2 Let heaven fill your thoughts. Do not think only about things down here on earth.

3 For you died when Christ died, and your real life is hidden with Christ in God.

4 And when Christ, who is your real life, is revealed to the whole world, you will share in all his glory.

Heaven is no afterthought. It is a place that has been deliberately and intentionally prepared for us by a God who has always loved us. In light of this truth, consider the following scriptures:

JEREMIAH 31:3

3   The Lord has appeared of old to me, saying: "Yes, I have loved you with an everlasting love; Therefore with loving-kindness I have drawn you."

MATTHEW 25:34

34   "Then the King will say to those on His right hand, 'Come, you blessed of My Father, inherit the kingdom prepared for you from the foundation of the world.'"

JOHN 14:1–3

1   "Let not your heart be troubled; you believe in God, believe also in Me.

2   "In My Father's house are many mansions; if it were not so, I would have told you. I go to prepare a place for you.

3   "And if I go and prepare a place for you, I will come again and receive you to Myself; that where I am, there you may be also."

JOHN 17:24 (New Living Translation)

24   Father, I want these whom you've given me to be with me, so they can see my glory. . . .

What a beautiful picture these scriptures paint! When you go to heaven, you will not be going as an unwelcome stranger, nor will you be merely "tolerated" as some type of divine concession. No! God has loved you with an everlasting love, and He has drawn you to Himself. He wants you to be with Him, and He has a Kingdom for you to inherit, a Kingdom that has been waiting for you from the foundation of the world. Jesus went to heaven with the specific intention of preparing a place for you!

God has not accepted us with reluctance or hesitation. Jesus said, *"Do not fear, little flock, for it is your Father's GOOD PLEASURE to give you the kingdom"* (Luke 12:32). God is happy that you and I will be in heaven with Him. As a matter of fact, when you and I repented of our sins and accepted Jesus as our Savior, there was a celebration in heaven! Jesus said, "... *There will be more joy in heaven over one sinner who repents than over ninety-nine just persons who need no repentance"* (Luke 15:7).

You are the object of God's eternal love! He will never stop loving you. He has loved you since before time began! There is nothing you can do to make God love you more than He already does, and there is nothing you could do to make Him love you less! Jesus loves you so much that He chose to die rather than have to live without you.

A LOOK AT THE AFTERLIFE
THROUGH 'HEAVEN'S WAITING ROOM'

Heaven was not always the place to which the departed spirits of the righteous went. In the Old Testament, the way to heaven had not yet been opened up. Righteous men in Old Testament times went to a temporary holding place, a place of comfort called Paradise, or Abraham's bosom. In a sense, it was like a waiting room where the righteous awaited the privilege of going into the very presence of God. This reality did not occur until Jesus had shed His blood, died, been raised from the dead, and ascended into heaven.

THE RICH MAN AND LAZARUS

Jesus shared the following story about a rich man and Lazarus to express truths concerning those who died.

LUKE 16:19–31

19 "There was a certain rich man who was clothed in purple and fine linen and fared sumptuously every day.

20 "But there was a certain beggar named Lazarus, full of sores, who was laid at his gate,

21 "desiring to be fed with the crumbs which fell from the rich man's table. Moreover the dogs came and licked his sores.

22 "So it was that the beggar died, and was carried by the angels to Abraham's bosom. The rich man also died and was buried.

23 "And being in torments in Hades, he lifted up his eyes and saw Abraham afar off, and Lazarus in his bosom.

24 "Then he cried and said, 'Father Abraham, have mercy on me, and send Lazarus that he may dip the tip of his finger in water and cool my tongue; for I am tormented in this flame.'

25 "But Abraham said, 'Son, remember that in your lifetime you received your good things, and likewise Lazarus evil things; but now he is comforted and you are tormented.

26 'And besides all this, between us and you there is a great gulf fixed, so that those who want to pass from here to you cannot, nor can those from there pass to us.'

27 "Then he said, 'I beg you therefore, father, that you would send him to my father's house,

28 'for I have five brothers, that he may testify to them, lest they also come to this place of torment.'

29 "Abraham said to him, 'They have Moses and the prophets; let them hear them.'

30 "And he said, 'No, father Abraham; but if one goes to them from the dead, they will repent.'

31 "But he said to him, 'If they do not hear Moses and the prophets, neither will they be persuaded though one rise from the dead.'"

Consider some of the lessons we can learn from Jesus' teaching:

The human body is buried, but the spirit goes elsewhere. In this passage, we see that the human body is buried at the time of death. However, the human spirit is not buried with the body. Rather, there are two possible destinations for the human spirit—one is a place of comfort; the other is a place of torment.

The spiritual man (even apart from the body) is a complete personality—possessing full consciousness, the ability to remember, the ability to recognize people, and so forth. Dr. W. A. Criswell, pastor for many years of First Baptist Church of Dallas, was once asked, "Will we know each other when we get to heaven?" He answered, "We won't really know each other until we get to heaven."[4]

Man's personality stays the same after death. Having been wealthy on earth, the rich man was accustomed to having servants and giving orders. Even after he died, he was trying to get Lazarus—a man of lesser status on earth—to carry out his wishes.

People who don't go to heaven have a strong desire for their living loved ones to accept God while they have the opportunity. The rich man realized there were things his brothers could do to change their destiny so theirs would not be the same as his. (This brings to mind a question that is often raised in pastoral ministry: People are often distraught when a loved one who died gave no evidence or indications of having accepted Jesus. Instead of assuming the worst, we must realize that we don't necessarily know what a person did in his final moments or seconds of consciousness—this means there is hope! The thief on the cross placed his faith in Jesus shortly before his death, and Jesus accepted him and assured him that he would be with Him in Paradise.)

PARADISE RELOCATED

Once Jesus died on the cross, was raised from the dead, and ascended into heaven, others could gain entrance into heaven. Jesus' redemptive work made it possible for the sins of man to be totally forgiven and enabled those who die to enter into God's presence in heaven.

Jesus' redemptive work also enabled the righteous who had already passed away and were in Paradise to enter into heaven. Ephesians 4:8 says, "When he ascended on high he led a host of captives . . ." (*RSV*). When Jesus ascended from the lower parts of the earth, He didn't ascend alone. He led with Him all of those righteous souls who had been comforted in Abraham's bosom. He took them to heaven with Him.

WHO IS IN HEAVEN AND WHAT WILL WE FIND THERE?

Having established that heaven is a real place, we can now address the question, "Who is in heaven and what will we find there?" Let's read what the Bible has to say on this subject.

The Book of Life Is In Heaven. There the names of God's children are written (Philippians 4:3; Revelation 21:27).

Magnificent Creatures Who Worship God Perpetually. There are magnificent creatures around God's throne that continually proclaim, *"Holy, holy, holy, Lord God Almighty, Who was and is and is to come!"* (Revelation 4:6–8).

Elders. There are elders who fall down before God in worship and cast their crowns of gold before the throne, saying, *"You are worthy, O Lord, to receive glory and honor and power; for You created all things, and by Your will they exist and were created"* (Revelation 4:10–11).

The Redeemed—Those Saved Through God's Mercy. Those who have been redeemed, purchased by the blood of Jesus, will be in heaven. These people will be from "all nations, tribes, peoples, and tongues" (Revelation 7:9). These cry out to the Lamb of God, "[You] *have made us kings* *and priests to our God; and we shall reign on the earth"* (Revelation 5:10).

The Apostle John, who was allowed by God to see heaven and record what he saw in the Book of Revelation, saw a large number of the redeemed in heaven. It wasn't just a few people from a specific denomination. John saw *"a great multitude which no one could number, of all nations, tribes, peoples, and tongues, standing before the throne and before the Lamb, clothed with white robes, with palm branches in their hands, and crying out with a loud voice, saying, 'Salvation belongs to our God who sits on the throne, and to the Lamb!'"* (Revelation 7:9–10).

Holy Angels. Angels are around the throne of God. John describes the number of them as "ten thousand times ten thousand, and thousands of thousands." These angels praise Jesus with a loud voice, saying, *"Worthy is the Lamb who was slain to receive power and riches and wisdom, and strength and honor and glory and blessing!"* (Revelation 5:11–12).

There is beauty and gloriousness in heaven beyond description. The Apostle John gave us the following details of heaven in the Book of Revelation.

- "The one sitting on the throne was as brilliant as gemstones—jasper and carnelian. And the glow of an emerald circled his throne like a rainbow" (Revelation 4:3 *NLT*).
- "In front of the throne was a shiny sea of glass, sparkling like crystal" (Revelation 4:6 *NLT*).
- "I saw before me what seemed to be a crystal sea mixed with fire" (Revelation 15:2 *NLT*).
- There is beautiful music in heaven. Revelation 14:2 and 3 says, "And I heard a sound from heaven like the roaring of a great waterfall or the rolling of mighty thunder. It was like the sound of many harpists playing together. This great

choir sang a wonderful new song in front of the throne of God . . ." (NLT).

- In heaven there are "living fountains of waters" (Revelation 7:17). And there is a "pure river of water of life, clear as crystal, proceeding from the throne of God and of the Lamb" (22:1).

- The "tree of life" is in heaven. John said that this tree "bore twelve fruits, each tree yielding its fruit every month. The leaves of the tree were for the healing of the nations" (Revelation 22:2).

- The New Jerusalem is described as "the holy city . . . descending out of heaven from God. It was filled with the glory of God and sparkled like a precious gem, crystal clear like jasper" (Revelation 21:10–11 NLT).

- The walls of the city are 216 feet thick (Revelation 21:17). The wall of this city has 12 foundation stones on which are written the names of the 12 apostles of the Lamb (21:14). The walls are made of jasper (21:18), and the foundation stones of the wall are inlaid with 12 different types of precious gems (21:19–20).

- There are 12 gates to the city, 3 on each side (north, south, east, and west), and an angel guards each gate. The names of the 12 tribes of Israel are written on the gates (Revelation 21:12–13). Each of the 12 gates is made from a single pearl (21:21). We are told the gates never close at the end of the day, because there is no night (21:25) and that nothing evil will be allowed to enter (21:27 NLT).

- The angel that was with John had a golden measuring stick. Revelation 21:16 says, "When he measured it, he found it was a square, as wide as it was long. In fact, it was in the form of a cube, for its length and width and height were each 1,400 miles" (NLT).

- Revelation 21:18 and 21 says, ". . . and the city was pure gold, as clear as glass. . . . And the main street was pure gold, as clear as glass" (*NLT*).

Leighton Ford is an evangelist who for many years worked as an associate to Billy Graham. His son Sandy died an untimely death, and in spite of his strong faith, Leighton struggled with that loss.

Even though he fully understood that he could not literally communicate with his departed son, Leighton kept a journal in which he wrote imaginary "conversations" with his son; it was his way of expressing things that were on the inside of him and bringing proper closure to the relationship.

In one of these imaginary conversations, Leighton wrote: "Sandy, you've been dead two months earthtime."

"I feel as if I have been alive forever, Dad. It's a lot like one big long today."

"It's not a matter of time, Sandy, except that time heals. It's more a matter of nearness. I guess I'm concerned that as our time goes on, we will lose any sense of nearness."

"But why, Dad? You're moving closer to eternity every day. You're no longer moving from, but to me! And besides, the 'Wall' between is so thin—you would laugh if you could see it."

"I think more of you than when you were at Chapel Hill."

"Sure! I know you do. I hear those thoughts."

"Night, son! Enjoy the stars!"

"It's morning here, Dad. Enjoy the light!"[5]

- According to Revelation 21:23, ". . . the city has no need of sun or moon, for the glory of God illuminates the city, and the Lamb is its light" (*NLT*).

These fantastic descriptions give us an inkling of who and what we will find in heaven.

WHAT WILL WE EXPERIENCE IN HEAVEN?

Besides the who and what of heaven, the Bible also tells us some of the experiences we will enjoy for eternity.

Perfect Reunion. Heaven is a place of perfect reunion. We will be reunited with loved ones, friends, and other believers who have gone before us.

1 THESSALONIANS 4:13–17

13 But I do not want you to be ignorant, brethren, concerning those who have fallen asleep, lest you sorrow as others who have no hope.

14 For if we believe that Jesus died and rose again, even so God will bring with Him those who sleep in Jesus.

15 For this we say to you by the word of the Lord, that we who are alive and remain until the coming of the Lord will by no means precede those who are asleep.

16 For the Lord Himself will descend from heaven with a shout, with the voice of an archangel, and with the trumpet of God. And the dead in Christ will rise first.

17 Then we who are alive and remain shall be caught up together with them in the clouds to meet the Lord in the air. And thus we shall always be with the Lord.

Notice, we will not be isolated from our loved ones who have preceded us in death, but we will be " *caught up together WITH THEM. . . . And thus we shall always be with the Lord*" (v. 17).

Perfect Transformation. Heaven is a place of perfect transformation. As we walk in the light of God's Word here on earth, we undergo a transformation. Paul said we are transformed by the renewing of our mind (Romans 12:2). However, what we experience here is partial and progressive. What we experience in heaven will be radical and absolute.

> **PSALM 17:15**
> 15 As for me, I will see Your face in righteousness; I shall be satisfied when I awake in Your likeness.

> **MATTHEW 13:43**
> 43 "Then the righteous will shine forth as the sun in the kingdom of their Father. He who has ears to hear, let him hear!"

> **1 JOHN 3:2**
> 2 Beloved, now we are children of God; and it has not yet been revealed what we shall be, but we know that when He is revealed, we shall be like Him, for we shall see Him as He is.

Perfect Comfort. Heaven offers perfect comfort. Thomas More said, "Earth hath no sorrow that heaven cannot heal." The Apostle John said, ". . . And he who sits on the throne will live among them and shelter them. They will never again be hungry or thirsty, and they will be fully protected from the scorching noontime heat. For the Lamb who stands in front of the throne will be their Shepherd. He will lead them to the springs of life-giving water. And God will wipe away all their tears" (Revelation 7:15–17 *NLT*).

Perfect Rejoicing, Gladness, and Joy. In heaven, there is an atmosphere of perfect rejoicing, gladness, and joy. Contrary to what some might think, heaven will not be a quiet place. There will be sounds of rejoicing throughout eternity.

REVELATION 19:6–7

6 And I heard, as it were, the voice of a great multitude, as the sound of many waters and as the sound of mighty thunderings, saying, "Alleluia! For the Lord God Omnipotent reigns!

7 "Let us be glad and rejoice and give Him glory, for the marriage of the Lamb has come, and His wife has made herself ready."

Perfect Fellowship and Feasting. In heaven, there will be perfect fellowship and feasting. Matthew 8:11 says, *"And I say to you that many will come from east and west, and sit down with Abraham, Isaac, and Jacob in the kingdom of heaven."* Revelation 19:9 says, *"Then he said to me, 'Write: "Blessed are those who are called to the marriage supper of the Lamb!"' And he said to me, 'These are the true sayings of God.'"*

A Perfect Inheritance. A perfect inheritance awaits believers in heaven. There is, *". . . an inheritance incorruptible and undefiled and that does not fade away, reserved in heaven for you"* (1 Peter 1:4).

Perfect Rest. Heaven is a place of perfect rest. Revelation 14:13 says, *"Then I heard a voice from heaven saying to me, 'Write: "Blessed are the dead who die in the Lord from now on."' 'Yes,' says the Spirit, 'that they may rest from their labors, and their works follow them.'"*

Perfect Rewards. God's nature is to reward His children. In order to be pleasing to God we *"must believe that He is, and that He is a rewarder of those who diligently seek Him"* (Hebrews 11:6). The Hebrew Christians were encouraged to work for the Lord, knowing that, *". . . God is not unjust to forget your work and labor of love which you have shown toward His name, in that you have ministered to the saints, and do minister"* (Hebrews 6:10).

There are many such scriptures that reveal God's plan to reward His children.

MATTHEW 5:12

12 . . . great is your reward in heaven.

MATTHEW 16:27

27 . . . He will reward each according to his works.

1 CORINTHIANS 3:14

14 If anyone's work which he has built on it endures, he will receive a reward.

2 TIMOTHY 4:8

8 . . . there is laid up for me the crown of righteousness, which the Lord, the righteous Judge, will give to me on that Day, and not to me only but also to all who have loved His appearing.

REVELATION 11:18

18 The nations were angry, and Your wrath has come, And the time of the dead, that they should be judged, And that You should reward Your servants the prophets and the saints, And those who fear Your name, small and great. . . . "

God's Perfect, Manifested Presence. When the New Jerusalem descends from heaven, God's perfect, manifested presence will be with His people. Revelation 21:3 and 4 says, *"And I heard a loud voice from heaven saying, 'Behold, the tabernacle of God is with men, and He will dwell with them, and they shall be His people. God Himself will be with them and be their God. And God will wipe away every tear from their eyes.'"*

Perfect Satisfaction. Heaven also offers perfect satisfaction. The fountain of the water of life is in heaven, and God invites all who thirst to drink freely (Revelation 21:6). Revelation 22:17 says, *"And the Spirit and the bride say, 'Come!' And let him who hears say, 'Come!' And let him who thirsts come. Whoever desires, let him take the water of life freely."*

Perfect Light. In heaven and in the New Jerusalem there will be perfect light.

REVELATION 21:10–11

10 And he carried me away in the Spirit to a great and high mountain, and showed me the great city, the holy Jerusalem, descending out of heaven from God,

11 having the glory of God. Her light was like a most precious stone, like a jasper stone, clear as crystal.

REVELATION 21:23–24

23 The city had no need of the sun or of the moon to shine in it, for the glory of God illuminated it. The Lamb is its light.

24 And the nations of those who are saved shall walk in its light, and the kings of the earth bring their glory and honor into it.

Perfect Government. Heaven is a place where God will reign in righteousness. There will be no corruption in His reign because His government shall be perfect.

REVELATION 19:6

6 And I heard, as it were, the voice of a great multitude, as the sound of many waters and as the sound of mighty thunderings, saying, "Alleluia! For the Lord God Omnipotent reigns!"

REVELATION 22:3

3 . . . the throne of God and of the Lamb shall be in it. . . .

Perfect Service. We do not know exactly all that our service will entail, but we will serve God in heaven.

> REVELATION 7:15 (New Living Translation)
> 15 . . . they are standing in front of the throne of God, serving him day and night in his Temple. . . .

> REVELATION 22:3
> 3 And there shall be no more curse, but the throne of God and of the Lamb shall be in it, AND HIS SERVANTS SHALL SERVE HIM.

Perfect Knowing. There will be perfect knowing in heaven. First Corinthians 13:12 says, *"For now we see in a mirror, dimly, but then face to face. Now I know in part, but then I shall know just as I also am known."*

Perfect Victory. In heaven, we will enjoy perfect victory—for eternity.

> REVELATION 3:21
> 21 "To him who overcomes I will grant to sit with Me on My throne, as I also overcame and sat down with My Father on His throne."

> REVELATION 22:5
> 5 There shall be no night there: They need no lamp nor light of the sun, for the Lord God gives them light. AND THEY SHALL REIGN FOREVER AND EVER.

The Absence of All Things Undesirable. There will be nothing undesirable, nothing evil, and nothing of sorrow in heaven.

REVELATION 7:16

16 They shall neither hunger anymore nor thirst anymore; the sun shall not strike them, nor any heat.

REVELATION 21:4

4 And God will wipe away every tear from their eyes; there shall be no more death, nor sorrow, nor crying. There shall be no more pain, for the former things have passed away.

REVELATION 21:25

25 . . . there shall be no night there.

REVELATION 21:27

27 But there shall by no means enter it anything that defiles, or causes an abomination or a lie . . .

REVELATION 22:3

3 And there shall be no more curse . . .

Imagine a world with no darkness, no danger, no decay, no deception, no depression, no despondency, no despair, no discouragement, no disappointment, no disillusionment, no disasters, no distress, no disturbances, no destruction, no defilement, no disease, no death, and no devil!

HEAVEN: NO EVIL—ONLY GOOD

In this wonderful place called heaven, there will be no evil, no wickedness, no unrighteousness, no ungodliness, and no sin. This is not wishful thinking—it is the world to which all of God's children are going. It is real, tangible, and eternal.

The heaven to which we are headed is a place without crime, without corruption, without pain, sorrows, and tears. There are no sirens, no deadbolts, and no alarm systems. There will be no barbed wire or razor wire. There is no adversity there, no trials, and no tribulation.

There are no ambulances, hospitals, cemeteries, or prisons. There are no plagues in heaven and no funerals. No one will be hungry or homeless, and earthquakes, tornadoes, hurricanes, floods, and raging fires will no longer exist to ravage mankind.

Heaven will be free from all sin, and there will be no temptation there. No one will be confused, and misunderstandings will simply not occur. No hateful words will ever be spoken there; crude, offensive behavior will not exist. Every motive of every person will be pure. Envy, covetousness, grudges, jealousies, and suspicions will be things of the distant past.

> There are a lot of questions the Bible doesn't answer about the Hereafter. But I think one reason is illustrated by the story of a boy sitting down to a bowl of spinach when there's a chocolate cake at the end of the table. He's going to have a rough time eating that spinach when his eyes are on the cake. And if the Lord had explained everything to us about what's ours to come, I think we'd have a rough time with our spinach down here.[6]
>
> —Vance Havner

There will be no abuse, exploitation, or violence in heaven, no strife and no broken hearts. No one will suffer from physical maladies, emotional disturbances, chemical imbalances, addictions, or handicaps of any kind—they simply won't exist in heaven. No one will be weary or exhausted. Worry, fear, and anxiety will not be present. All bondages that afflicted and tormented people on earth will have been absolutely vanquished—eliminated entirely!

I understand that even in this world we have victory through Jesus. It is true that we are more than conquerors through Him who loved us (Romans 8:37). But isn't it exhilarating to know that the day is coming when we won't have to fight and contend with earthly challenges anymore? All battles will be over, all opposition removed, and nothing will remain except celebration, rejoicing, and absolute glory!

We can and should draw enormous strength from knowing what is ahead of us. The Apostle Paul put it this way:

2 CORINTHIANS 4:16–18 (*New Living Translation*)

16 That is why we never give up. Though our bodies are dying, our spirits are being renewed every day.

17 For our present troubles are quite small and won't last very long. Yet they produce for us an immeasurably great glory that will last forever!

18 So we don't look at the troubles we can see right now; rather, we look forward to what we have not yet seen. For the troubles we see will soon be over, but the joys to come will last forever.

In our physical body, we have physical eyes and other senses to perceive what is happening in the natural world around us. But God has also given us "eyes of faith" to see that which cannot be perceived with the physical senses. In embracing the truths and promises of God's Word, the Holy Spirit quickens these wonderful things to our heart, creating enthusiastic anticipation about the realities that are ahead of us.

RUNNING OUR RACE; REACHING FOR HEAVEN

Perhaps while reading this chapter on heaven, you have thought of loved ones who have already gone home to be with the Lord. They have been experiencing firsthand the wonders of heaven—things you and I can only imagine. You may be facing challenges in your life, but I believe those who have gone before us are cheering us on from the grandstands of heaven.

HEBREWS 12:1–4 (*The Living Bible*)

1 Since we have such a huge crowd of men of faith watching us from the grandstands, let us strip off anything that slows us down or holds us back, and especially those sins that wrap themselves so tightly around our feet and trip us up; and let us run with patience the particular race that God has set before us.

2 Keep your eyes on Jesus, our leader and instructor. He was willing to die a shameful death on the cross because of the joy he knew would be his afterwards; and now he sits in the place of honor by the throne of God.

3 If you want to keep from becoming fainthearted and weary, think about his patience as sinful men did such terrible things to him.

4 After all, you have never yet struggled against sin and temptation until you sweat great drops of blood.

1 PETER 5:8–11

8 Be sober, be vigilant; because your adversary the devil walks about like a roaring lion, seeking whom he may devour.

9 Resist him, steadfast in the faith, knowing that the same sufferings are experienced by your brotherhood in the world.

10 But may the God of all grace, who called us to His eternal glory by Christ Jesus, after you have suffered a while, perfect, establish, strengthen, and settle you.

11 To Him be the glory and the dominion forever and ever. Amen.

As believers in Jesus, we have the eternal hope of being established, strengthened, and settled in Christ. We can run the race set before us with perseverance, knowing that Jesus is both the Author and the Finisher of our faith.

Thoughts of heaven quicken our faith. Our only sure and solid foundation is the hope of heaven. The only solution to earth's mysteries, the only righter of earth's wrongs, and the only cure for worldliness, is heaven. We need an infusion of heaven into our faith and hope that will create a homesickness for that blessed place. God's home is heaven. Eternal life and all good were born there and flourish there. All life, happiness, beauty, and glory are native to the home of God. All this belongs to and awaits the heirs of God in heaven. What a glorious inheritance![7]

God's promise of heaven should have a major influence in the way we live our lives here on earth. We have no reason to be pessimistic or fatalistic about our future. How we think, what we believe, what our attitude is, and how we conduct ourselves here should all be affected by the reality of heaven that is before us. The hope of heaven is what enables us to live our lives and deal with death according to an eternal perspective.

[1] *The New Encyclopedia of Christian Quotations* comp. Mark Water (Grand Rapids, Mich.: Baker Books, 2000), p. 469.

[2] *The New Encyclopedia of Christian Quotations*, p. 469. Used by permission of The C.S. Lewis Company Ltd.

[3] C.S. Lewis, *Mere Christianity* (New York: HarperCollins Publishers, 2001), pp. 136–137. Used by permission of The C.S. Lewis Company Ltd.

[4] Michael P. Green, ed., *Illustrations for Biblical Preaching* (Grand Rapids, Mich.: Baker Book House, 1989), p. 184.

[5] Leighton Ford, *Sandy, a Heart for God* (Downers Grove, Ill.: InterVarsity Press, 1985), p. 171. Used by permission of the author.

[6] *Illustrations for Biblical Preaching*, p. 184.

[7] E.M. Bounds, *The Promise of Heaven: A Kingdom, a Crown & an Inheritance* (Greenville, S.C.: Ambassador, 2001), pp. 50–51. Used by permission of Ambassador Publications.

chapter 13

ETERNAL LIFE: KNOW WHERE YOU'RE GOING

The most important issue you will ever face in life pertains to where you will spend eternity. For many years, this matter of eternity was unresolved in my own life. I was raised in church, believed in God, and tried to be a good person. I believed heaven existed, and I hoped to go there when I died. However, I lacked the assurance of *knowing* that I had eternal life and would spend eternity in heaven.

Part of the problem was that I wasn't sure what it took to get into heaven. Like many people, I assumed that acceptance by God was largely based on my own works and efforts. In other words, I believed that if I was good enough, God would let me into heaven. But there was a nagging concern that maybe I wasn't quite good enough. After all, I really didn't know exactly what "good enough" was as far as God was concerned.

WHAT DOES THE BIBLE SAY?

Eventually I saw some wonderful truths in the Bible that answered my questions and enabled me to receive God's gift of eternal life.

1. God loves us and does not want us to perish.

John 3:16 and 17 says, *"For God so loved the world that He gave His only begotten Son, that whoev*er believes in Him should not perish but have everlasting life. For God did not send His Son into the world to condemn the world, but that the world through Him might be saved."* First Timothy 2:4 says, *"*[God] *desires all men to be saved and to come to the knowledge of the truth."*

2. All people have sinned. Sin causes separation from God.

According to Isaiah 59:2, our iniquities have separated us from God, and our sins have hidden His face from us. Romans 3:23 says, *"For all have sinned and fall short of the glory of God."* And James 2:10 says, *"For whoever shall keep the whole law, and yet stumble in one point, he is guilty of all."*

3. Heaven is a free gift. You cannot earn or deserve heaven.

Romans 6:23 tells us that the wages of sin is death, but the gift of God is eternal life in Christ Jesus. Ephesians 2:8 and 9 says, *"For by grace you have been saved through faith, and that not of yourselves; it is the gift of God, not of works, lest anyone should boast."*

4. God wanted us to be brought back into relationship with Him. For this reason, Jesus paid the penalty for our sin when He died upon the cross.

According to Romans 5:8 and 9, God demonstrated His love for us *"in that while we were still sinners, Christ died for us. Much more then, having now been justified by His blood, we shall be saved from wrath through Him."* First Corinthians 15:3 tells us that Christ died for our sins.

5. We receive God's forgiveness through faith, which means trusting in Christ.

John 1:12 says, *"But as many as received Him, to them He gave the right to become children of God, to those who believe in His name."* Romans chapter 10 tells us exactly how to express our faith in Christ in order to receive salvation: *". . . if you confess with your mouth the Lord Jesus and believe in your heart that God has raised Him from the dead, you will be saved. For with the heart one believes unto righteousness, and with the mouth confession is made unto salvation"* (vv. 9–10).

The Bible makes it clear that God loves us so much that He sent Jesus to die in our place in order to bridge the gap caused by sin and to reconcile us to the Father. God's Word also clearly tells us how to accept this free gift of salvation and eternal life. But there is *more* good news—we don't have to wait a lifetime to accept this gift!

YOU CAN RECEIVE THIS GIFT RIGHT NOW!

You can place your faith in Jesus and receive God's gift of eternal life *right now*. I encourage you to agree with God's Word and to express your faith in God by praying the following prayer:

Dear God,

I come to You and acknowledge that I have sinned. I need Your mercy and Your forgiveness. I turn to You now, and I repent of my sins.

I believe that Your Son Jesus came to this earth and died on the cross for my sins. I believe that He rose from the dead so that I could receive forgiveness and the gift of eternal life. I accept Jesus as my Savior, and I confess Him now as my Lord.

Thank You for taking away my sins, for making me Your child, and for placing me in right standing with You.

In Jesus' Name I pray. Amen.

NOW THAT YOU'VE RECEIVED
THE GIFT OF ETERNAL LIFE . . .

Realize that in receiving the gift of eternal life, you have taken a wonderful spiritual step. God not only wants you to have this gift, but He also wants you to get to know Him, to follow Him, and to serve Him with your whole heart. There are several practical steps you can take in order to better accomplish these things.

Step 1. One practical step I suggest you take to get to know your heavenly Father better and to build a relationship with Him is to get a Bible and begin reading it. I recommend beginning with the Gospel of John. This particular book of the Bible offers a tremendous introduction to who Jesus is. I also recommend you read a Bible that is translated into modern language. You might consider the *New King James Version* or the *New Living Translation*.

Step 2. Another practical step to take to build your relationship with your heavenly Father involves finding a good church and attending regularly. It is important to become a part of a church that believes in the Lordship of Jesus, the authority of the Bible, and the power of the Holy Spirit. Your spiritual walk and your spiritual growth can be greatly helped by your involvement in a strong local church.

Step 3. While the Holy Spirit already lives in you once you accept Jesus as your Savior, there is an additional experience by which He fills you with power. This important step of receiving the gift of the Holy Spirit is part of God's plan for your life. In the Bible, you can read all about the outstanding works of the Holy Spirit in the Book of Acts.

Step 4. Another step following salvation is to be baptized in water. Baptism is an outward demonstration of an inward reality. In other words, it signifies the fact that you have become identified with the death, burial, and resurrection of Jesus Christ. The Book of Acts records numerous instances of early Christians being baptized in water in obedience to the instructions of Jesus.

IF YOU ARE TEMPTED TO DOUBT . . .

If you are ever tempted to doubt the fact that you are now a child of God and will spend eternity with Him, know that the Bible has many tremendous promises to further assure you. Here are three scriptures that are especially comforting:

JOHN 5:24

24 "Most assuredly, I say to you, he who hears My word and believes in Him who sent Me has everlasting life, and shall not come into judgment, but has passed from death into life."

JOHN 6:37

37 "All that the Father gives Me will come to Me, and the one who comes to Me I will by no means cast out."

1 JOHN 5:13

13 These things I have written to you who believe in the name of the Son of God, that you may know that you have eternal life, and that you may continue to believe in the name of the Son of God.

Don't allow negative thoughts, lies from the devil, or the words of other people to steal your confidence. You are a child of God—and you will spend eternity with Him!

LET US HEAR FROM YOU!

If you prayed the prayer earlier in this chapter for the first time, or if you have rededicated your life to the Lord, please contact us through our ministry Web site—**www.tonycooke.org**—and let us know. We'd love to hear from you!

chapter 14

THE GLORIOUS RESURRECTION

In the midst of deep frustration and turmoil, Job asked the question, "If a man dies, shall he live again?" (Job 14:14). To this question, the Bible responds with a resounding and triumphant, *"Yes!"*

The idea of one's spirit, or inward man, going to heaven is very comforting, but it is far from the total picture painted in the Scriptures. The Bible's teaching does not ignore or eliminate any part of a person from its place in God's eternal plan. The human body is a vital part of who a person is—just as the intellectual, emotional, and spiritual faculties are a vital part.

Some people have mistakenly thought that the afterlife consists of vapor-like spirits floating around the clouds. The fact is, though, that God created human beings as whole people—spirit, soul, and body—and that is exactly how we will live throughout eternity.

As previously explained, there is definitely a time, or season, following death when we will be "absent from the body." However, there is a further dimension involving our physical body as part of our eternal state, or condition. This brings us to the Bible's teaching regarding the resurrection.

A GLORIOUS REUNION

The word "resurrection" is from the Greek word *anastasis* which is literally translated "to make to stand" or "rise up." It is defined as *the reunion of the bodies and souls of men that have been separated by death.*[1]

Perhaps the earliest biblical reference to a physical life after death was made by Job in the midst of his sufferings.

JOB 19:25–26

25 For I know that my Redeemer lives, And He shall stand at last on the earth;

26 And after my skin is destroyed, this I know, That in my flesh I shall see God.

Various prophets of the Old Testament also alluded to the resurrection:

Isaiah said, ". . . your dead will live; their bodies will rise. You who dwell in the dust, wake up and shout for joy. . . . the earth will give birth to her dead" (Isaiah 26:19 *NIV*).

Hosea said, "I will ransom them from the power of the grave; I will redeem them from death . . ." (Hosea 13:14 *NIV*).

Daniel said, *"And many of those who sleep in the dust of the earth shall awake, Some to everlasting life, Some to shame and everlasting contempt"* (Daniel 12:2).

NEW TESTAMENT PROOF OF A RESURRECTION

In the New Testament, the teaching concerning the resurrection becomes even more vivid and powerful. Jesus said to the Jews, *"Most assuredly, I say to you, the hour is coming, and now is, when the dead will hear the voice of the Son of*

THE GLORIOUS RESURRECTION

God; and those who hear will live. Do not marvel at this; for the hour is coming in which all who are in the graves will hear His voice and come forth—those who have done good, to the resurrection of life, and those who have done evil, to the resurrection of condemnation" (John 5:25,28–29).

> The Hebrews had a wonderful faith in God, but only glimmers of understanding of the fullness of life after death. God's revelation of the meaning of death and life reached its fulfillment in the resurrection of Jesus Christ from the dead. His resurrection revealed a genuine continuity with His earthly life and yet also a total transformation, heralding a life beyond the physical creation. He is the foretaste of a new creation, the hope of every believer; his resurrection is the pattern of our resurrection.[2]

The Apostle Paul stated, *". . . we ourselves groan within ourselves, eagerly waiting for the adoption, the redemption of our body"* (Romans 8:23). *Paul further stated, "For our citizenship is in heaven, from which we also eagerly wait for the Savior, the Lord Jesus Christ, who will transform our lowly body that it may be conformed to His glorious body . . ."* (Philippians 3:20–21).

The Bible makes it clear that something very positive will happen to our physical body in the future.

> This hope is closely connected with his promised return to this earth, when, in the Apostle John's words, "we shall be like him for we shall see him as he is." The Christian's hope of heaven is more than a return to the paradise of Eden, it is a new creation with new depths of personal relationship with God and with one another.[3]

To embrace this truth requires faith in the promises and faithfulness of God, especially since we perceive with our physical senses that our body is getting older, and we know that our body will eventually die (see 2 Corinthians 4:16).

Author Philip Yancey wrote the following:
I know a woman whose grandmother lies buried under 150-year-old live oak trees in the cemetery of an Episcopal church in rural Louisiana. In accordance with the grandmother's instructions, only one word is carved on the tombstone: "Waiting."[4]

The Bible's most extensive teaching on the resurrection of the body is found in First Corinthians chapter 15.

1 CORINTHIANS 15:51–54
51 Behold, I tell you a mystery: We shall not all sleep, but we shall all be changed—
52 in a moment, in the twinkling of an eye, at the last trumpet. For the trumpet will sound, and the dead will be raised incorruptible, and we shall be changed.
53 For this corruptible must put on incorruption, and this mortal must put on immortality.
54 So when this corruptible has put on incorruption, and this mortal has put on immortality, then shall be brought to pass the saying that is written: "Death is swallowed up in victory."

In First Corinthians chapter 15 Paul establishes the historic reality of Christ's resurrection as the foundation for the future resurrection of every believer. These two events (Christ's resurrection and our own) are inextricably connected. In reference to resurrection, Jesus is called "Christ the firstfruits"

(1 Corinthians 15:20,23) and "the firstborn from the dead" (Colossians 1:18; Revelation 1:5). By this we know that our resurrection as believers will be like the resurrection experienced by the Lord Jesus Christ. His resurrection was a bodily resurrection and the prototype for what we will experience.

> Benjamin Franklin wrote in advance the epitaph to be on his gravestone: "The body of Benjamin Franklin, Printer, like the cover of an old book, its contents torn out and stripped of its lettering and gilding, lies here . . . Yet the Work itself shall not be lost; for it will, as he believed, appear once more in a new and more beautiful edition, corrected and amended by the Author."[5]

WHEN WILL THE RESURRECTION TAKE PLACE?

When will we experience this bodily resurrection? First Thessalonians 4:13–18, a passage frequently read at graveside services, gives us some answers.

1 THESSALONIANS 4:13–18

13 But I do not want you to be ignorant, brethren, concerning those who have fallen asleep, lest you sorrow as others who have no hope.

14 For if we believe that Jesus died and rose again, even so God will bring with Him those who sleep in Jesus.

15 For this we say to you by the word of the Lord, that we who are alive and remain until the coming of the Lord will by no means precede those who are asleep.

16 For the Lord Himself will descend from heaven with a shout, with the voice of an archangel, and with the trumpet of God. And the dead in Christ will rise first.

17 Then we who are alive and remain shall be caught up together with them in the clouds to meet the Lord in the air. And thus we shall always be with the Lord.

18 Therefore comfort one another with these words.

There are two dimensions (spirit and body) involved in the resurrection, both of which are mentioned in this passage. On one hand, *"God will bring with Him those who sleep in Jesus"* (v. 14). This refers to the spirits of people who are currently in heaven. We know they are in heaven (and not "sleeping" where their body was buried in the earth) because this passage says they will return *as God brings them with Him.*

The second dimension is the physical dimension. Verse 16 says, *"The dead in Christ will rise first,"* referring to the *physical body* of those who had already died. What takes place in the resurrection (for those who have already died) is a reuniting of the spirit and body, which were separated at death.

At the resurrection, our corruptible and mortal bodies are made incorruptible and immortal by the power of God. God will transform our lowly body that it may be conformed to His glorious body (Philippians 3:21). The Bible teaches two wonderful, parallel truths: our spirits are immortal, and our bodies will be resurrected.

IN THE END . . .

The Church Age will be brought to a close with the resurrection. In Revelation 20:6, John says, *"Blessed and holy is he who has part in the first resurrection. Over such the second death has no power, but they shall be priests of God and of Christ, and shall reign with Him a thousand years."* God created us as whole people—spirit, soul, and body—and that is exactly how we will live during the millennium, the thousand-year reign of Christ upon this earth, and throughout all eternity.

Charles Spurgeon said, "When we shall rise again, we shall be freed from all corruption; no evil tendencies shall remain in us . . . . 'Without spot or wrinkle, or any such thing,' without even the shadow of a spot which the eye of Omniscience could discover, we shall be as pure as Adam before his fall, as holy as the Immaculate manhood when it first came from the divine hand. We shall be better than Adam, for Adam might sin, but we shall be so established in goodness, in truth, and in righteousness, that we shall not even be tempted again, much less shall we have any fear of falling. We shall stand spotless and faultless at the last great day. Brethren, lift up your heads."[6]

Many Christians, so persuaded of heaven and the future resurrection, see an element of celebration in death. Rather than view it as the end, they rightly chose to see death for what it is . . . *a new beginning.*

Billy Graham, at the funeral of Richard Nixon, related the story of how Winston Churchill planned his own funeral with the hope of the resurrection in mind. Churchill instructed that after the benediction a bugler, positioned high in the dome of St. Paul's Cathedral, play "Taps"—the universal signal indicating that the day is over. But then came the most dramatic part. Churchill instructed that another bugler, on the other side of the dome, play the notes of "Reveille"—the universal signal that a new day has dawned and it's time to arise. So Churchill was testifying that at the end of history the last note will not be "Taps" but "Reveille." There is hope beyond the grave because Christ has opened to us the door of heaven and new life by his own death and resurrection.[7]

When the reality of the resurrection becomes alive inside of us, our inevitable death will no longer be the last word. We can know with confidence that a glorious reunion awaits us at the resurrection. We will receive a glorified body—a body free of sickness, pain, and deterioration—with which to enjoy eternity with God. Knowing this with certainty, we can rejoice in sorrow, awaiting our resurrection and the resurrection of our loved ones.

When it comes to dealing with the loss of a loved one, grieving, and moving on in life—not one of us is an expert. We are seldom prepared and rarely ready to say good-bye. We somehow imagined that our loved ones would live forever. Perhaps that is because eternity has been imprinted upon our hearts. Truly, we will live forever—that is the confident hope that steadies us in times of sorrow. An eternity with our Savior, with our Creator and God, and with our loved ones and friends—that is the joy set before us.

[1] Merrill F. Unger, *The New Unger's Bible Dictionary*, Revised and updated edition, ed. R.K. Harrison and cont. eds. Howard F. Vos and Cyril J. Barber (Chicago: Moody Press, 1988), p. 1075.

[2] Bruce Nicholls, "We All Believe Something," *Eerdman's Handbook to Christian Belief*, org. ed. Robin Keeley (Oxford: Lion Publishing plc, 1982; 1st American Edition 1982, William B. Eerdmans Publishing Co., Grand Rapids, Mich.), p. 35.

[3] Nicholls, Eerdman's Handbook to Christian Belief, p. 35.

[4] Taken from **JESUS I NEVER KNEW, The – Hardcover** by PHILIP D. YANCEY, p. 275. Copyright © 1995 by Philip Yancey. Used by permission of Zondervan.

[5] Taken from *Encyclopedia of 7,700 Illustrations* by Paul Lee Tan © Bible Communications, Inc. [www.tanbible.com] (Chicago: Assurance Publishers, 1979), p. 312.

[6] Charles Haddon Spurgeon, *Sermons of Rev. C.H. Spurgeon of London*, Vol. 7 (1883; reprinted as Spurgeon's Sermons, Grand Rapids, Mich.: Baker Book House), p. 370 (page citation is to the reprint edition).

[7] Paul E. Engle, ed., *Baker's Funeral Handbook: Resources for Pastors* (Grand Rapids, Mich.: Baker Books, 1996), p. 164.

TOO YOUNG TO DIE

Typically, we can understand, at least intellectually, when an older person dies. We usually accept the passing of someone who has lived a long, full life. However, it seems so contrary to the natural order of things when a child dies or when an infant is stillborn.

The impact of a child's death on parents is so traumatic that an estimated seventy to eighty percent of those marriages result in divorce.[1] A wise pastor or counselor, along with supportive friends, family members, and a church family can be of great benefit in providing support to the parents whose child has died.

GENDER DIFFERENCES IN THE GRIEVING PROCESS

Very often, men and women react to loss differently. The variance in how each responds can be a source of tension, friction, and frustration. Over time, men will often intellectually and analytically size up the situation, realize there is nothing that can be done to change the circumstances, and move on. A woman's tendency can be to approach the situation emotionally, contemplate and grieve the loss, and then back off for a season. This process may then be repeated many, many times: approaching, backing off, and then approaching the situation again.

While the man may just want to "forget it and move forward," the woman finds therapeutic value in talking often about the situation. This is where problems may occur. The man can become irritated and frustrated, feeling as though his wife wants to keep rehashing the same information over and over. The woman can feel rejected since her husband does not eagerly engage in talking with her about matters that are very near and dear to her heart.

It has been said that men typically communicate on a factual level, for the sake of exchanging information. However, communication for women is an emotional experience, and they talk for the sake of building closeness.

Please keep in mind that all of this is very generalized information, and it is not assumed to be absolutely true for every individual or couple. It has also been presented very simplistically, and I realize that human dynamics can be far more complicated than what has just been described. However, many couples will be able to relate to this description to one degree or another. When my wife and I experienced a miscarriage many years ago, we experienced some of these dynamics ourselves.

WE LOOK FOR ANSWERS

We feel a great need to find answers for the important questions that arise when dealing with miscarriages and stillbirths. What happens to a baby's spirit upon death? Do babies go to heaven? What about a baby that never lives outside his or her mother's womb? The Word of God makes some very powerful statements about God's hand and power in the formation of a baby even before birth.

PSALM 139:13–16 (*New Living Translation*)

13 You made all the delicate, inner parts of my body and knit me together in my mother's womb.

14 Thank you for making me so wonderfully complex! Your workmanship is marvelous—and how well I know it.

15 You watched me as I was being formed in utter seclusion, as I was woven together in the dark of the womb.

16 You saw me before I was born. Every day of my life was recorded in your book. Every moment was laid out before a single day had passed.

To both the Prophet Jeremiah and the Apostle Paul, God spoke of the fact that He knew them and had called them before they were born.

JEREMIAH 1:5

5 "Before I formed you in the womb I knew you; Before you were born I sanctified you . . . ."

GALATIANS 1:15

15 But when it pleased God, who separated me from my mother's womb and called me through His grace.

Consider also the amazing account of John the Baptist being filled with the Holy Spirit while still in his mother's womb. Also, when Elizabeth was pregnant with John the Baptist, and when Mary was pregnant with Jesus, the two women met together. It is fascinating that John the Baptist, while yet in Elizabeth's womb, leapt for joy as soon as Elizabeth heard Mary's voice.

LUKE 1:13–15,39–45

13 But the angel said to him, "Do not be afraid, Zacharias, for your prayer is heard; and your wife Elizabeth will bear you a son, and you shall call his name John.

14 "And you will have joy and gladness, and many will rejoice at his birth.

15 "For he will be great in the sight of the Lord, and shall drink neither wine nor strong drink. He will also be filled with the Holy Spirit, even from his mother's womb. . . ."

39 Now Mary arose in those days and went into the hill country with haste, to a city of Judah,

40 and entered the house of Zacharias and greeted Elizabeth.

41 And it happened, when Elizabeth heard the greeting of Mary, that the babe leaped in her womb; and Elizabeth was filled with the Holy Spirit.

42 Then she spoke out with a loud voice and said, "Blessed are you among women, and blessed is the fruit of your womb!

43 "But why is this granted to me, that the mother of my Lord should come to me?

44 "For indeed, as soon as the voice of your greeting sounded in my ears, the babe leaped in my womb for joy.

45 "Blessed is she who believed, for there will be a fulfillment of those things which were told her from the Lord."

It is comforting to see in Scripture that God knows each child while he or she is being formed in the womb. For parents who have experienced the death of a child, the attitude that Jesus displayed toward children can also be tremendously comforting.

MARK 10:13–16

13 Then they brought little children to Him, that He might touch them; but the disciples rebuked those who brought them.

14 But when Jesus saw it, He was greatly displeased and said to them, "Let the little children come to Me, and do not forbid them; for of such is the kingdom of God.

15 "Assuredly, I say to you, whoever does not receive the kingdom of God as a little child will by no means enter it."
16 And He took them up in His arms, put His hands on them, and blessed them.

Remember that the Bible teaches us that Jesus is the same yesterday, today, and forever (Hebrews 13:8). If Jesus embraced and accepted little children when He was alive on this earth, I have no doubt that He does the same today in heaven.

ARE BABIES SAVED?

Some people will wonder how babies or children can go to heaven when they have never heard the Gospel or accepted Jesus for themselves. I believe Paul shed light on this subject when he wrote, *"I was alive once without the law, but when the commandment came, sin revived and I died"* (Romans 7:9). The only time that Paul would have been "without the law" was when he was a very young child.

Paul said he was "alive" at the time when he was too young to comprehend biblical teaching. This can't be in reference to physical life, because he was alive physically both before and after learning God's Word. He didn't die physically when he came to the knowledge of the law. However, before he learned the law—before he had the knowledge of God's commandments and of right and wrong—Paul was *spiritually* alive, or spiritually united to God.

When Paul was old enough to learn the commandments of God, he realized that he had sinned and had violated God's commandments. It was at this time according to Romans 7:9 that Paul died spiritually—became spiritually separated from

God—and was thus in need of accepting Jesus as his Savior in order to be reunited with God. This age of awareness is often called the *age of accountability*. It refers to the age at which a young person becomes old enough to be responsible for responding to the truth of God's Word.

> "No little child has ever come from God and stayed a brief while, returning again to the Father, without making glad the home, and leaving behind some trace of heaven."[2]
>
> —John Watson

Only God knows the age of accountability for each person, but certainly miscarried or stillborn children, as well as very young children who die, are far from the age of awareness. I believe that these children are safely in heaven with God.

Although the death of a child—whether by miscarriage, stillbirth, or premature death—is difficult to comprehend with our human reasoning, the Holy Spirit offers comfort and strength to help us through our sorrow. And even though we may not understand everything, we can be confident in God's mercy and compassion. The good news of God's mercy is simply this: Jesus loved, embraced, and welcomed children to Himself when He was here on this earth, and Jesus is the same yesterday, today, and forever (Hebrews 13:8).

[1] Crisis Counseling, rev. ed., by H. Norman Wright. Copyright 1993 by Gospel Light/Regal Books, Ventura, CA 93003. Used by permission.

[2] James L. Christensen, *Difficult Funeral Services* (Old Tappan, N.J.: Fleming H. Revell Company, 1985), p. 99.

SPIRITUALISM: TALKING WITH THE DEAD?

For centuries, people have sought to establish contact and communicate with their deceased loved ones. Today, spiritualism takes the form of television entertainment as mediums (people through whom the dead supposedly speak) convey alleged messages from dead relatives and friends to fascinated and awe-struck members of the viewing audience.

This practice may appear on the surface to be comforting and helpful, but the Bible very strongly and specifically denounces it. Consider the following scriptures:

LEVITICUS 19:26,31

26 "You shall not eat anything with the blood, nor shall you practice divination or soothsaying. . . .

31 "Give no regard to mediums and familiar spirits; do not seek after them, to be defiled by them: I am the Lord your God."

The *New Living Translation* renders these verses, " 'Never eat meat that has not been drained of its blood. 'Do not practice fortune-telling or witchcraft. . . . 'Do not rely on mediums and psychics, for you will be defiled by them. I, the Lord, am your God.' " In these verses, God through Moses addressed a collection of pagan practices connected with superstition and magic. One commentary summarized these verses by saying, "The Israelites were to abstain from all unnatural, idolatrous, and heathenish conduct."[1]

The Old Testament contains many passages that teach against the practice of spiritualism and other forms of witchcraft and divination.

LEVITICUS 20:6–7

6 "And the person who turns to mediums and familiar spirits, to prostitute himself with them, I will set My face against that person and cut him off from his people.

7 "Consecrate yourselves therefore, and be holy, for I am the Lord your God."

DEUTERONOMY 18:9–14

9 "When you come into the land which the Lord your God is giving you, you shall not learn to follow the abominations of those nations.

10 "There shall not be found among you anyone who makes his son or his daughter pass through the fire, or one who practices witchcraft, or a soothsayer, or one who interprets omens, or a sorcerer,

11 "or one who conjures spells, or a medium, or a spiritist, or one who calls up the dead.

12 "For all who do these things are an abomination to the Lord, and because of these abominations the Lord your God drives them out from before you.

13 "You shall be blameless before the Lord your God.

14 "For these nations which you will dispossess listened to soothsayers and diviners; but as for you, the Lord your God has not appointed such for you."

ISAIAH 8:19–20

19 And when they say to you, "Seek those who are mediums and wizards, who whisper and mutter," should not a people seek their God? Should they seek the dead on behalf of the living?

20 To the law and to the testimony! If they do not speak according to this word, it is because there is no light in them.

ISAIAH 8:19–20 (The Living Bible)

19 So why are you trying to find out the future by consulting witches and mediums? Don't listen to their whisperings and mutterings. Can the living find out the future from the dead? Why not ask your God?

20 "Check these witches' words against the Word of God!" he says. "If their messages are different than mine, it is because I have not sent them; for they have no light or truth in them."

In the New Testament, Jesus made a very strong point that helps us understand why God's people are not to seek communication with the dead. In Luke 16:19–30, Jesus told the story of two men. The rich man in this story died and went to hell. Lazarus also died and was carried by the angels into paradise, or "Abraham's bosom" as it is referred to in these verses. Notice the requests made by the rich man.

LUKE 16:24–31

24 "Then he cried and said, 'Father Abraham, have mercy on me, and send Lazarus that he may dip the tip of his finger in water and cool my tongue; for I am tormented in this flame.'

25 "But Abraham said, 'Son, remember that in your lifetime you received your good things, and likewise Lazarus evil things; but now he is comforted and you are tormented.

26 'And besides all this, between us and you there is a great gulf fixed, so that those who want to pass from here to you cannot, nor can those from there pass to us.'

27 "Then he said, 'I beg you therefore, father, that you would send him to my father's house,

28 'for I have five brothers, that he may testify to them, lest they also come to this place of torment.'

29 "Abraham said to him, 'They have Moses and the prophets; let them hear them.'

30 "And he said, 'No, father Abraham; but if one goes to them from the dead, they will repent.'

31 "But he said to him, 'If they do not hear Moses and the prophets, neither will they be persuaded though one rise from the dead.'"

From this passage we learn that when people die, their spirits are not at liberty to wander around and take care of unfinished business. According to the Bible, when a human spirit leaves its body, it goes to heaven or to hell. The dead are not free to roam around wherever they want. We also see that the deceased rich man wanted Lazarus, who had also died, to send a message to the rich man's still-living relatives. Abraham did not hesitate in stating that such permission would not be granted. (It is interesting that the rich man did not ask if he himself could go—it appears that he had an intuitive awareness that he was not going anywhere. However, he may have thought that someone else might be able to go.)

HUMAN DECEPTION
OR SUPERNATURAL FACTORS?

Any appearance of spiritualism being authentic is rooted in human deception or demonic manifestations. What do we mean by human deception? There are people who are talented in manipulating others. They make general suggestions and then work off of the responses of people. Observers should also be aware that people can be planted in an audience who will work with the medium or psychic according to a pre-arranged script.

In addition to natural explanations, there can also be supernatural factors involved in spiritualism. In the Bible, the Holy Spirit occasionally passed on certain information to His servants—we call this receiving "a word of knowledge" (1 Corinthians 12:8). But not only can the Holy Spirit pass information to men; evil spirits can pass information also.

Consider what happened in Philippi in conjunction with the ministry of the Apostle Paul:

ACTS 16:16–19 (New Living Translation)
16 One day as we were going down to the place of prayer, we met a demon-possessed slave girl. She was a fortune-teller who earned a lot of money for her masters.
17 She followed along behind us shouting, "These men are servants of the Most High God, and they have come to tell you how to be saved."
18 This went on day after day until Paul got so exasperated that he turned and spoke to the demon within her. "I command you in the name of Jesus Christ to come out of her," he said. And instantly it left her.
19 Her masters' hopes of wealth were now shattered, so they grabbed Paul and Silas and dragged them before the authorities at the marketplace.

It is obvious from this story that the abilities of this girl were more than natural in origin. When the evil spirit was cast out of her, she was no longer able to perform her psychic activities.

Involvement with fortune-telling, magic, psychics, séances, or conversations with the dead places the believer on extremely dangerous ground! This is why the Bible explicitly forbids God's children to become involved in any way in the occult. God's command that we not speak to the dead is not given because God is mean or wants to deny us meaningful interaction with our deceased loved ones.

God tells us the truth for our benefit. He has a way for us to interact with our deceased loved ones, but it is His way, on His terms, and in His timing. When we acknowledge that our loved ones are in another realm and that communication with them will not take place until we are together in heaven, we are exhibiting patience and are submitting to God's revealed truth. Impatience and rebellion, believing that we can circumvent God's established ways, will only lead to trouble.

The Christian must be on guard against deception. Paul was very concerned about the gullibility of the Corinthians, and he warned them against falling prey to false and deceptive influences.

2 CORINTHIANS 11:13–15

13 For such are false apostles, deceitful workers, transforming themselves into apostles of Christ.

14 And no wonder! For Satan himself transforms himself into an angel of light.

15 Therefore it is no great thing if his ministers also transform themselves into ministers of righteousness, whose end will be according to their works.

John shared Paul's concern for those to whom he ministered, and he instructed believers to "not believe every spirit, but test the spirits, whether they are of God" (1 John 4:1).

ARE THERE ANY EXCEPTIONS?

Have there ever been exceptions to this rule—the principle that there is no communication between the living and the dead? I believe so. First Samuel chapter 28 provides the strange account of King Saul endeavoring to establish contact with the deceased prophet Samuel. The very exceptional nature of this event is accentuated in the final pronouncement of judgment that came upon Saul's failed life and leadership. First Chronicles 10:13 says, *"So Saul died for his unfaithfulness which he had committed against the Lord, because he did not keep the word of the Lord, and also because he consulted a medium for guidance."*

Yes, a supernatural encounter took place, but it was by no means the norm; it is certainly not an example to be imitated by others.

JESUS SPOKE TO MOSES AND ELIJAH ON THE MOUNT OF TRANSFIGURATION

The other biblical exception to God's prohibition against communication with the dead took place in the life of Jesus Himself. While Saul's experience followed a pattern of disobedience, Jesus' encounter with Moses and Elijah came in the midst of His life of perfect obedience (see Luke 9:28–31). Just as Jesus' death on the cross for the sins of the world was not the norm, neither was His experience of conversing with men who had died. Romans 14:9 tells us that Jesus is Lord of both the dead and the living. Even though Jesus is our example in many ways, we must acknowledge that He is the unique, one-of-a-kind Son of God.

As Christians, we must live our life in line with the Word of God. This means that we do not follow or embrace spiritualists who claim to have supernatural messages for us from deceased loved ones, even if those spiritualists claim their gift is from God.

1 THESSALONIANS 5:19–22

19 Do not quench the Spirit.

20 Do not despise prophecies.

21 Test all things; hold fast what is good.

22 Abstain from every form of evil.

The Apostle Paul admonished believers to be discerning and discriminating even about prophecies within the church—messages that brought simple comfort, edification, and exhortation and were supposedly of heavenly origin.

The believer's hope is not in getting information from a psychic. Our hope is in the promises and revealed truth of God's Word. This involves patience. It involves recognizing that our loved one is living in a realm separate from ours. We will see him or her again, but it will be in the place that God appoints and in the way that God designed. As the old hymn of the church says, "What a day of rejoicing that will be!"

---

[1] From Keil & Delitzsch, *Commentary on the Old Testament: New Updated Edition,* Electronic Database. Copyright © 1996 by Hendrickson Publishers, Inc., Peabody, Mass.

DEALING WITH SUICIDE

One of the most difficult situations a person can face is having a loved one commit suicide. In addition to dealing with an intensified form of normal grief issues (guilt, anger, confusion, and so forth), surviving family members frequently feel isolated from friends and others in their church and community. They may feel a sense of shame about the manner of their loved one's death and simply not know what to say or how to explain the situation. Those who would normally offer support to the family may also feel uncomfortable about the situation. They may keep their distance due to their awkward feelings and their own difficulty of not knowing what to say.

Early in ministry, I was approached by a man who told me he had been having an ongoing debate with his friend about what happened to the spirit of a Christian who committed suicide. He asked my opinion. Taking his question at face value, I stressed the mercy of God in my answer. Little did I realize that within a couple of weeks, this active member of the church would take his own life. I answered his question entirely from an *after-the-fact* perspective, never realizing his hidden despair or knowing that what he needed to hear was information from a *preventive* perspective.

Had this man been forthcoming about his challenges, intervention could have taken place. Prayer, counsel, medical help, or other needed forms of ministry and support could have been marshaled for his benefit to help him overcome the sense of hopelessness and helplessness that plagued him. Even with intervention, this man still would have had to make the decision to live, but the support could have made a difference. Instead, his life was cut short, and many people were left hurting and confused in the wake of his death.

While I strongly believe in stressing the mercy of God whenever possible to a family *after* a suicide has occurred, I also strongly believe we should stress God's will concerning the act of suicide if there is still an opportunity to *prevent* a suicide from taking place.

HOW TO APPROACH THE SUBJECT OF SUICIDE

In addressing the subject, two distinct perspectives can be taken, depending upon whether or not a suicide has taken place: the *after-the-fact* perspective and the *preventive* perspective. We minister differently to those who are contemplating suicide than we do to those who are grieving the loss of a loved one who has already committed suicide.

For a person contemplating suicide, it is important to understand that suicide is not the will of God for His children.

FIVE BIBLICAL PRINCIPLES CONCERNING SUICIDE

We will look at five biblical principles that reinforce the fact that suicide is not God's will.

1. Suicide is a violation of God's commandment against murder. The sixth commandment, found in Exodus 20:13, says, "Thou shalt not kill" (*KJV*). This verse is literally translated, "Thou shalt not commit murder,"[1] and reads similarly in the *New King James Version* and the *New International Version*. Suicide is the murder of one's self.

2. Suicide is a violation of God's commandment that we love ourselves. When asked which was the greatest commandment in the Law, Jesus responded: *"'You shall love the Lord your God with all your heart, with all your soul, and with all your mind.' "This is the first and great commandment. "And the second is like it: 'You shall love your neighbor as yourself'"* (Matthew 22:37–39). In addition to having a biblical responsibility to love our neighbor, we also have a responsibility to love ourselves. If a person loves himself, he will not destroy himself. Suicide is an act of self-abhorrence.

3. Suicide is a violation of God's commandment that we honor our bodies as His temple. First Corinthians 6:19 and 20 says, *"Or do you not know that your body is the temple of the Holy Spirit who is in you, whom you have from God, and you are not your own? For you were bought at a price; therefore glorify God in your body and in your spirit, which are God's."* A person does not have the right to destroy someone else's property. We do not own our body; therefore it is not ours to destroy. However, we are stewards of our body, and we have a mandate from God to glorify Him in our body.

4. Suicide is contrary to God's plan that our life be a blessing to other people. Romans 13:10 says, *"Love does no harm to a neighbor; therefore love is the fulfillment of the law."* Suicide brings enormous grief, heartache, and sorrow to surviving family and friends. In this sense, suicide damages more than just the victim. It does great harm to others, and it is actually an ultimate act of selfishness.

5. Suicide is contrary to the fulfilling of God's plan for our life. Jeremiah 29:11 says, *"For I know the thoughts that I think toward you, says the Lord, thoughts of peace and not of evil, to give you a future and a hope."* No one can receive or fulfill the plan of God for his life if he removes himself from the earth by suicide. God is a God of hope, and suicide represents the abandonment of hope. Thus, suicide is a means of rejecting the purpose of God for one's life.

SCRIPTURAL EXAMPLES OF SUICIDE

Although the act of suicide is clearly against God's Word, the Bible provides various examples of people who committed suicide—none of which is edifying.

- Saul and his armor bearer took their own lives by falling on their swords at the end of a losing battle (1 Samuel 31:4–5).

- Ahithophel, a government advisor, felt deeply spurned when his counsel was rejected so he hanged himself (2 Samuel 17:23).

- Judas Iscariot hanged himself after betraying Jesus (Matthew 27:5).

While the Bible records these accounts of suicide, they in no way represent an example of godly behavior. Like various other ungodly deeds recorded in the Bible, these instances are written for our instruction, so we can learn what *not to do* in addition to learning what to do.

IS THERE A PLACE FOR MERCY?

For those who have already had a family member commit suicide, their concerns must be addressed with compassion. While it demonstrates insensitivity to lecture the bereaved on biblical principles against suicide, it is quite appropriate to talk with them about God's great mercy.

Surviving family members often have legitimate and sincere questions about the spirit of the person who took his own life. There is no doubt that suicide is contrary to God's will and God's intentions for the lives of people, but survivors—those left behind following a suicide—can still look to God for mercy and grace. Consider the following:

Years ago, I was asked to conduct a funeral service for a young man who had committed suicide. He had a long history of mental illness. In speaking with the family, I learned that his mental condition caused him oftentimes to be out of touch with reality. It was during one of these episodes that he took his life.

The family asked that I directly address the issue of suicide and mental illness at the funeral. While praying and studying in preparation for this particular funeral message, I came across a fascinating statement that Jesus made on the cross. Jesus prayed, "Father, forgive them, for they don't know what they do" (Luke 23:34). I told those gathered that I was not trying to play the role of God, but that I did see reason for hope. If Jesus could extend mercy and forgiveness toward those who didn't know what they were doing 2,000 years ago, couldn't we expect him to also extend mercy and forgiveness today to someone whose judgment was severely impaired due to a mental illness?

Rev. Kenneth E. Hagin shared the following story concerning his own mother:

> My father left home when I was six. My mother, because of all the problems she'd had with him, had a complete nervous and physical breakdown. So we went to live with our grandparents on her side of the family.
>
> When Granny had to be doing something, such as hanging out the clothes to dry, she would have me watch Momma. Momma had "spells" when she would want to kill herself. I had to watch to see that she didn't get hold of a knife or something dangerous. That made quite an impression on me as a young child.
>
> . . . My mother was a Christian—but just a baby Christian. She knew Christ as her Savior, but she did not know how to

stand, and so on. What if she had killed herself? Would she have been saved? Well, it is possible to be sick in your head just as much as it is possible to be sick in your stomach. Would someone go to hell just because he was sick in his stomach? No. Nor would he go to hell just because he was sick in his head. Being sick in his head would not keep him from going to heaven.

People can be sick in their heads and not even know what they are doing. Momma lived to be 80. Years after she recovered and I was in the ministry, I suddenly began to talk to her one day about having had to watch her and some of those things. "Why, Son, don't you ever say a thing like that," she said. "You know I'm a Christian. I wouldn't have done anything like that. I wouldn't have taken my own life." She had no knowledge of it whatever. I never mentioned it to her again. . . .

Even we could tell when one of those terrible attacks was coming. She would go into a preliminary attack of depression. She would get to thinking about everything that ever had happened to her in life. You see, her parents had not wanted her to marry my father. . . . When Momma married him against her parents' wishes, she said, "If I make my bed hard, I'll lie on it." She made her bed hard, and she tried to lie on it. But she just could not make it.

If you are not careful, you can get to thinking about the past—mistakes you made, where you missed it—and get depressed. Then you can get into a spirit of depression. And that opens the door to the devil. You can get so perplexed and depressed and oppressed until you do not know what you are doing, which direction you are going, and hardly what your name is.[2]

Ultimately, we must leave each person's eternal destiny in God's hands. You are not the Judge, and neither am I. It is not our responsibility to make the call as to how God will judge each particular person. We may know certain things about what went on externally, but we don't know all that went on inside of a particular person. Only God truly knows all the facts. While we never seek to justify suicide, we must also recognize that we are not necessarily aware of the pressures, the pain, or the perceptions that were present within an individual. As with any kind of death, we must simply commit the spirit of an individual who took his life into the hands of an all-knowing, righteous, and merciful God.

---

[1] Jamieson, Fausset, and Brown Commentary, Electronic Database. Copyright © 1997 by Biblesoft.

[2] Kenneth E. Hagin, *What To Do When Faith Seems Weak & Victory Lost* (Tulsa: Faith Library Publications, 1979), pp. 19–21.

RAISING THE DEAD

When a loved one dies, the family may want that person back *right then*—not in a promised future resurrection. Confronted with extreme sorrow, everything within them may resist death's reality and seek to reverse it. The bereaved may see only one course of action: to receive a miracle from God and have their loved one come back to life.

People who know the promises of God concerning the here and now are inclined to have very optimistic faith in God's ability to perform the miraculous. After all, they state, it was Jesus Himself who said, *"The things which are impossible with men are possible with God"* (Luke 18:27).

I have seen families faced with imminent death overwhelmingly desire that their loved one receive healing and not die. Some even said the Lord told them that their loved one would recover. After their loved one died, they then became adamant that God was going to raise him or her from the dead. When their loved one did not come back to life, the families had to deal with additional issues. Not only was there the unfortunate loss of their loved one, but to compound matters, they then had to deal with the additional disappointment of not having their loved one raised from the dead. They also perhaps had to face the embarrassment of having made certain "faith statements" to others that did not come to pass.

Did God let them down? Did their faith fail? After all, they were sure He had spoken to them! In ministering in these situations, I have encouraged families not to be hard on themselves. They are not to be faulted for believing that the Holy Spirit spoke a specific word to them. When people are in a state of emotional upheaval, it can be difficult to discern between "God having spoken" and what was simply an intense emotional desire for a loved one to live. Instead of feeling *condemned*, a family can realize that their great love for the person who died is to be *commended*.

As honorable as it is to have an intense desire to see someone we love continue with us, it is also necessary sometimes to release that person to the care of God in heaven. Recognizing our human limitations is a part of life. There are times when we come face-to-face with the realization that we cannot control every person and every circumstance. However, we can choose to place and keep our trust in God no matter what. God is God, and He always will be God, regardless of the outcome of any specific situation.

LET'S CONSIDER THE FACTS

I believe strongly in God's power to heal. I know people who are alive and well today after doctors said they would die. I have also seen situations that did not turn out the way others and I would have liked.

What about raising the dead? I've heard stories about the dead being supernaturally raised by the power of God in modern times, and I do not doubt for a moment that God can and still does perform such miracles. However, I think it is important to look at the big picture. With the Bible as our guide, I believe we should determine if the dead being raised is the normal experience or if it is a very exceptional miracle.

The Bible records a mere 8 specific instances of an individual being raised from the dead as a result of the faith, prayers, or ministry of another person. With the Bible covering history over a 4,500-year period, that is an average of only 1 person being raised from the dead every 562.5 years. Even in Bible days, the dead being raised was not an everyday occurrence but a very exceptional miracle. The instances of the dead being raised in the Bible include:

- The widow's son through the ministry of Elijah (1 Kings 17:17–24).
- The son of the Shunammite couple through the ministry of Elisha (2 Kings 4:8–37).
- The dead man being buried whose corpse touched the bones of Elisha (2 Kings 13:20–21).
- The daughter of Jairus through the ministry of Jesus (Matthew 9:18–19,23–26).
- The son of the widow in Nain through the ministry of Jesus (Luke 7:11–16).
- Lazarus through the ministry of Jesus (John 11:1–44).
- Dorcas through Peter's ministry (Acts 9:36–42).
- Eutychus through the ministry of Paul (Acts 20:7–12).

While I do not believe that the days of miracles have passed away, I see no basis to believe that the dead being raised is going to transition from being a fairly uncommon experience in Bible days to being an extremely frequent experience in modern times.

WHY IS THE MIRACLE OF RAISING THE DEAD SO EXCEPTIONAL?

If raising the dead were merely contingent upon a family's desire to have their loved one back, the dead would be raised regularly. If we could simply "believe that we receive" our dead relatives back to life, the dead would be raised all the

215

time. In short, human will or desire will not bring the dead back to life. The raising of the dead is an exceptional miracle, and it involves an exceptional work of the Holy Spirit.

The Apostle Paul taught about the working of the Holy Spirit in First Corinthians chapter 12. Consider these Spirit-breathed words:

1 CORINTHIANS 12:4–11

4 There are diversities of gifts, but the same Spirit.

5 There are differences of ministries, but the same Lord.

6 And there are diversities of activities, but it is the same God who works all in all.

7 But the manifestation of the Spirit is given to each one for the profit of all:

8 for to one is given the word of wisdom through the Spirit, to another the word of knowledge through the same Spirit,

9 to another faith by the same Spirit, to another gifts of healings by the same Spirit,

10 to another the working of miracles, to another prophecy, to another discerning of spirits, to another different kinds of tongues, to another the interpretation of tongues.

11 But one and the same Spirit works all these things, distributing to each one individually as He wills.

1 CORINTHIANS 12:9–10 (*Amplified*)

9 To another [wonder-working] faith by the same [Holy] Spirit, to another the extraordinary powers of healing by the one Spirit;

10 To another the working of miracles. . . .

I believe that in order for the dead to be raised, there must be three distinct manifestations of the Holy Spirit taking place simultaneously (keep in mind that Paul said these manifestations of the Holy Spirit operate as the Spirit wills).

First, *the gift of special faith* must be in operation. General, ordinary faith is not sufficient to raise the dead—if it was, we would see the dead raised frequently and commonly.

Second, there must be *a gift* (or *gifts*) *of healings* in operation. If the person raised from the dead did not receive an outstanding healing, the sickness that took his life the first time would still be present and would very quickly take his life again.

Third, *the working of miracles* is necessary in order for the dead to be raised. What is a miracle? A miracle involves a divine and supernatural intervention that changes the ordinary course of nature.

If you desired for your loved one to be raised from the dead and were disappointed, you don't need to feel ashamed or condemned. Your love for your loved one is commendable. David, the Sweet Psalmist of Israel and the one called "a man after God's own heart," came to a painful but necessary realization when he said regarding his dead son, *"But now he is dead; why should I fast? Can I bring him back again? I shall go to him, but he shall not return to me"* (2 Samuel 12:23). While David realized he could not bring his son back to life, his heart was filled with the knowledge that he would one day join his son in heaven.

Our loved one's death may not be the outcome we would have desired, but death is the conclusion to this earthly life, and we will all reach it at one point or another if the Lord tarries His return. Even so, it is a conclusion that we accept with the accompanying presence of the Holy Spirit, and with the assurance of a future reunion in glory.

SCRIPTURES OF COMFORT AND STRENGTH

Throughout the ages, men and women of faith have turned to the Word of God to be a source of guidance, strength, and comfort. This chapter contains various scriptures that I pray will be of great help during times of sorrow. When heartache, confusion, or loneliness threaten to overwhelm you, remember the promise of Psalm 62:7, which says, "In God is my salvation and my glory; the rock of my strength, and my refuge, is in God."

EXODUS 34:6–7
6 And the Lord passed before him and proclaimed, "The Lord, the Lord God, merciful and gracious, longsuffering, and abounding in goodness and truth,
7 "keeping mercy for thousands, forgiving iniquity and transgression and sin. . . ."

NUMBERS 6:24–26
24 "'The Lord bless you and keep you;
25 The Lord make His face shine upon you, And be gracious to you;
26 The Lord lift up His countenance upon you, And give you peace.'"

DEUTERONOMY 7:9

9 Therefore know that the Lord your God, He is God, the faithful God who keeps covenant and mercy for a thousand generations with those who love Him and keep His commandments.

DEUTERONOMY 29:29

29 "The secret things belong to the Lord our God, but those things which are revealed belong to us and to our children forever, that we may do all the words of this law."

DEUTERONOMY 33:27

27 The eternal God is your refuge, And underneath are the everlasting arms. . . .

JOB 19:25–27

25 For I know that my Redeemer lives, And He shall stand at last on the earth;

26 And after my skin is destroyed, this I know, That in my flesh I shall see God,

27 Whom I shall see for myself, And my eyes shall behold, and not another. How my heart yearns within me!

PSALM 12:5

5 "For the oppression of the poor, for the sighing of the needy, Now I will arise," says the Lord; "I will set him in the safety for which he yearns."

PSALM 18:4–6,16–19

4 The pangs of death surrounded me, And the floods of ungodliness made me afraid.

5 The sorrows of Sheol surrounded me; The snares of death confronted me.

6 In my distress I called upon the Lord, And cried out to my God; He heard my voice from His temple, And my cry came before Him, even to His ears. . . .

16 He sent from above, He took me; He drew me out of many waters.

17 He delivered me from my strong enemy, From those who hated me, For they were too strong for me.

18 They confronted me in the day of my calamity, But the Lord was my support.

19 He also brought me out into a broad place; He delivered me because He delighted in me.

PSALM 23:1–6

1 The Lord is my shepherd; I shall not want.

2 He makes me to lie down in green pastures; He leads me beside the still waters.

3 He restores my soul; He leads me in the paths of righteousness For His name's sake.

4 Yea, though I walk through the valley of the shadow of death, I will fear no evil; For You are with me; Your rod and Your staff, they comfort me.

5 You prepare a table before me in the presence of my enemies; You anoint my head with oil; My cup runs over.

6 Surely goodness and mercy shall follow me All the days of my life; And I will dwell in the house of the Lord Forever.

PSALM 27:13–14

13 I would have lost heart, unless I had believed That I would see the goodness of the Lord in the land of the living.

14 Wait on the Lord; Be of good courage, And He shall strengthen your heart; Wait, I say, on the Lord!

PSALM 28:8–9

8 The Lord is their strength, And He is the saving refuge of His anointed.

9 Save Your people, And bless Your inheritance; Shepherd them also, and bear them up forever.

PSALM 29:11

11 The Lord will give strength to His people; The Lord will bless His people with peace.

PSALM 30:10–12

10 "Hear, O Lord, and have mercy on me; Lord, be my helper!"

11 You have turned for me my mourning into dancing; You have put off my sackcloth and clothed me with gladness,

12 To the end that my glory may sing praise to You and not be silent. O Lord my God, I will give thanks to You forever.

PSALM 31:24

24 Be of good courage, And He shall strengthen your heart, All you who hope in the Lord.

PSALM 32:7

7 You are my hiding place; You shall preserve me from trouble; You shall surround me with songs of deliverance.

PSALM 34:17–19

17 The righteous cry out, and the Lord hears, And delivers them out of all their troubles.

18 The Lord is near to those who have a broken heart, And saves such as have a contrite spirit.

19 Many are the afflictions of the righteous, But the Lord delivers him out of them all.

PSALM 42:1–3,5

1 As the deer pants for the water brooks, So pants my soul for You, O God.

2 My soul thirsts for God, for the living God. When shall I come and appear before God?

3 My tears have been my food day and night, While they continually say to me, "Where is your God?" . . .

5 Why are you cast down, O my soul? And why are you disquieted within me? Hope in God, for I shall yet praise Him For the help of His countenance.

PSALM 46:1–2

1 God is our refuge and strength, A very present help in trouble.

2 Therefore we will not fear, Even though the earth be removed, And though the mountains be carried into the midst of the sea.

PSALM 48:14

14 For this is God, Our God forever and ever; He will be our guide Even to death.

PSALM 56:8–10 (New Living Translation)

8 You keep track of all my sorrows. You have collected all my tears in your bottle. You have recorded each one in your book.

9 On the very day I call to you for help, my enemies will retreat. This I know: God is on my side.

10 O God, I praise your word. Yes, Lord, I praise your word.

PSALM 57:1

1 Be merciful to me, O God, be merciful to me! For my soul trusts in You; And in the shadow of Your wings I will make my refuge, Until these calamities have passed by.

PSALM 61:1–4

1 Hear my cry, O God; Attend to my prayer.

2 From the end of the earth I will cry to You, When my heart is overwhelmed; Lead me to the rock that is higher than I.

3 For You have been a shelter for me, A strong tower from the enemy.

4 I will abide in Your tabernacle forever; I will trust in the shelter of Your wings.

PSALM 62:1–2,5–8

1 Truly my soul silently waits for God; From Him comes my salvation.

2 He only is my rock and my salvation; He is my defense; I shall not be greatly moved. . . .

5 My soul, wait silently for God alone, For my expectation is from Him.

6 He only is my rock and my salvation; He is my defense; I shall not be moved.

7 In God is my salvation and my glory; The rock of my strength, And my refuge, is in God.

8 Trust in Him at all times, you people; Pour out your heart before Him; God is a refuge for us.

PSALM 71:3,5,14

3 Be my strong refuge, To which I may resort continually; You have given the commandment to save me, For You are my rock and my fortress. . . .

5 For You are my hope, O Lord God; You are my trust from my youth. . . .

14 But I will hope continually, And will praise You yet more and more.

PSALM 73:25–26

25 Whom have I in heaven but You? And there is none upon earth that I desire besides You.

26 My flesh and my heart fail; But God is the strength of my heart and my portion forever.

PSALM 84:1–12 (*American Standard Version*)

1 How amiable are thy tabernacles, O Jehovah of hosts!

2 My soul longeth, yea, even fainteth for the courts of Jehovah; My heart and my flesh cry out unto the living God.

3 Yea, the sparrow hath found her a house, And the swallow a nest for herself, where she may lay her young, Even thine altars, O Jehovah of hosts, My King, and my God.

4   Blessed are they that dwell in thy house: They will be still praising thee.

5   Blessed is the man whose strength is in thee; In whose heart are the highways to Zion.

6   Passing through the valley of Weeping they make it a place of springs; Yea, the early rain covereth it with blessings.

7   They go from strength to strength; Every one of them appeareth before God in Zion.

8   O Jehovah God of hosts, hear my prayer; Give ear, O God of Jacob.

9   Behold, O God our shield, And look upon the face of thine anointed.

10 For a day in thy courts is better than a thousand. I had rather be a doorkeeper in the house of my God, Than to dwell in the tents of wickedness.

11 For Jehovah God is a sun and a shield: Jehovah will give grace and glory; No good thing will he withhold from them that walk uprightly.

12 O Jehovah of hosts, Blessed is the man that trusteth in thee.

PSALM 91:1–4

1   He who dwells in the secret place of the Most High Shall abide under the shadow of the Almighty.

2   I will say of the Lord, "He is my refuge and my fortress; My God, in Him I will trust."

3   Surely He shall deliver you from the snare of the fowler And from the perilous pestilence.

4   He shall cover you with His feathers, And under His wings you shall take refuge; His truth shall be your shield and buckler.

PSALM 92:1–2

1   It is good to give thanks to the Lord, And to sing praises to Your name, O Most High;

2   To declare Your lovingkindness in the morning, And Your faithfulness every night.

PSALM 94:17–19

17 Unless the Lord had been my help, My soul would soon have settled in silence.

18 If I say, "My foot slips," Your mercy, O Lord, will hold me up.

19 In the multitude of my anxieties within me, Your comforts delight my soul.

PSALM 103:8,11–12

8 The Lord is merciful and gracious, Slow to anger, and abounding in mercy. . . .

11 For as the heavens are high above the earth, So great is His mercy toward those who fear Him;

12 As far as the east is from the west, So far has He removed our transgressions from us.

PSALM 116:5–8,12–19

5 Gracious is the Lord, and righteous; Yes, our God is merciful.

6 The Lord preserves the simple; I was brought low, and He saved me.

7 Return to your rest, O my soul, For the Lord has dealt bountifully with you.

8 For You have delivered my soul from death, My eyes from tears, And my feet from falling. . . .

12 What shall I render to the Lord For all His benefits toward me?

13 I will take up the cup of salvation, And call upon the name of the Lord.

14 I will pay my vows to the Lord Now in the presence of all His people.

15 Precious in the sight of the Lord Is the death of His saints.

16 O Lord, truly I am Your servant; I am Your servant, the son of Your maidservant; You have loosed my bonds.

17 I will offer to You the sacrifice of thanksgiving, And will call upon the name of the Lord.

18 I will pay my vows to the Lord Now in the presence of all His people,

19 In the courts of the Lord's house, In the midst of you, O Jerusalem. Praise the Lord!

PSALM 130:3–7

3 If You, Lord, should mark iniquities, O Lord, who could stand?

4 But there is forgiveness with You, That You may be feared.

5 I wait for the Lord, my soul waits, And in His word I do hope.

6 My soul waits for the Lord More than those who watch for the morning—Yes, more than those who watch for the morning.

7 O Israel, hope in the Lord; For with the Lord there is mercy, And with Him is abundant redemption.

PSALM 145:8–9

8 The Lord is gracious and full of compassion, Slow to anger and great in mercy.

9 The Lord is good to all, And His tender mercies are over all His works.

PROVERBS 3:5–6

5 Trust in the Lord with all your heart, And lean not on your own understanding;

6 In all your ways acknowledge Him, And He shall direct your paths.

PROVERBS 14:32

32 . . . the righteous has a refuge in his death.

PROVERBS 18:10

10 The name of the Lord is a strong tower; the righteous run to it and are safe.

ISAIAH 25:6–8 (*New Living Translation*)

6 In Jerusalem, the Lord Almighty will spread a wonderful feast for everyone around the world. It will be a delicious feast of good food, with clear, well-aged wine and choice beef.

7 In that day he will remove the cloud of gloom, the shadow of death that hangs over the earth.

8 He will swallow up death forever! The Sovereign Lord will wipe away all tears. He will remove forever all insults and mockery against his land and people. The Lord has spoken!

ISAIAH 40:11,28–31

11 He will feed His flock like a shepherd; He will gather the lambs with His arm, And carry them in His bosom, And gently lead those who are with young. . . .

28 Have you not known? Have you not heard? The everlasting God, the Lord, The Creator of the ends of the earth, Neither faints nor is weary. His understanding is unsearchable.

29 He gives power to the weak, And to those who have no might He increases strength.

30 Even the youths shall faint and be weary, And the young men shall utterly fall,

31 But those who wait on the Lord Shall renew their strength; They shall mount up with wings like eagles, They shall run and not be weary, They shall walk and not faint.

ISAIAH 41:10

10 Fear not, for I am with you; Be not dismayed, for I am your God. I will strengthen you, Yes, I will help you, I will uphold you with My righteous right hand.

ISAIAH 43:1–2

1 But now, thus says the Lord, who created you, O Jacob, And He who formed you, O Israel: "Fear not, for I have redeemed you; I have called you by your name; You are Mine.

2 When you pass through the waters, I will be with you; And through the rivers, they shall not overflow you. When you walk through the fire, you shall not be burned, Nor shall the flame scorch you."

ISAIAH 46:4 (New Living Translation)

4 I will be your God throughout your lifetime—until your hair is white with age. I made you, and I will care for you. I will carry you along and save you.

ISAIAH 49:15–16

15 "Can a woman forget her nursing child, And not have compassion on the son of her womb? Surely they may forget, Yet I will not forget you.

16 See, I have inscribed you on the palms of My hands; Your walls are continually before Me."

ISAIAH 51:11–12

11 So the ransomed of the Lord shall return, And come to Zion with singing, With everlasting joy on their heads. They shall obtain joy and gladness; Sorrow and sighing shall flee away.

12 "I, even I, am He who comforts you. Who are you that you should be afraid Of a man who will die, And of the son of a man who will be made like grass?"

ISAIAH 54:10

10 "For the mountains shall depart And the hills be removed, But My kindness shall not depart from you, Nor shall My covenant of peace be removed," Says the Lord, who has mercy on you.

ISAIAH 57:1–2 (New Living Translation)

1 The righteous pass away; the godly often die before their time. And no one seems to care or wonder why. No one seems to understand that God is protecting them from the evil to come.

2 For the godly who die will rest in peace.

ISAIAH 60:20

20 Your sun shall no longer go down, Nor shall your moon withdraw itself; For the Lord will be your everlasting light, And the days of your mourning shall be ended.

ISAIAH 61:1–3

1 "The Spirit of the Lord God is upon Me, Because the Lord has anointed Me To preach good tidings to the poor; He has sent Me to heal the brokenhearted, To proclaim liberty to the captives, And the opening of the prison to those who are bound;

2 "To proclaim the acceptable year of the Lord, And the day of vengeance of our God; To comfort all who mourn,

3 "To console those who mourn in Zion, To give them beauty for ashes, The oil of joy for mourning, The garment of praise for the spirit of heaviness; That they may be called trees of righteousness, The planting of the Lord, that He may be glorified."

JEREMIAH 17:7–8

7 "Blessed is the man who trusts in the Lord, And whose hope is the Lord.

8 For he shall be like a tree planted by the waters, Which spreads out its roots by the river, And will not fear when heat comes; But its leaf will be green, And will not be anxious in the year of drought, Nor will cease from yielding fruit."

JEREMIAH 29:11,13

11 For I know the thoughts that I think toward you, says the Lord, thoughts of peace and not of evil, to give you a future and a hope. . . .

13 And you will seek Me and find Me, when you search for Me with all your heart.

LAMENTATIONS 3:22–24

22 Through the Lord's mercies we are not consumed, Because His compassions fail not.

23 They are new every morning; Great is Your faithfulness.

24 "The Lord is my portion," says my soul, "Therefore I hope in Him!"

MATTHEW 5:4

4 Blessed are those who mourn, For they shall be comforted.

MATTHEW 11:28–30

28 "Come to Me, all you who labor and are heavy laden, and I will give you rest.

29 "Take My yoke upon you and learn from Me, for I am gentle and lowly in heart, and you will find rest for your souls.

30 "For My yoke is easy and My burden is light."

JOHN 5:24–30

24 "Most assuredly, I say to you, he who hears My word and believes in Him who sent Me has everlasting life, and shall not come into judgment, but has passed from death into life.

25 "Most assuredly, I say to you, the hour is coming, and now is, when the dead will hear the voice of the Son of God; and those who hear will live.

26 "For as the Father has life in Himself, so He has granted the Son to have life in Himself,

27 "and has given Him authority to execute judgment also, because He is the Son of Man.

28 "Do not marvel at this; for the hour is coming in which all who are in the graves will hear His voice

29 "and come forth—those who have done good, to the resurrection of life, and those who have done evil, to the resurrection of condemnation.

30 "I can of Myself do nothing. As I hear, I judge; and My judgment is righteous, because I do not seek My own will but the will of the Father who sent Me."

JOHN 6:37 (Amplified)

37 All whom My Father gives (entrusts) to Me will come to Me; and the one who comes to Me I will most certainly not cast out [I will never, no never, reject one of them who comes to Me].

JOHN 10:27–29

27 "My sheep hear My voice, and I know them, and they follow Me.

28 "And I give them eternal life, and they shall never perish; neither shall anyone snatch them out of My hand.

29 "My Father, who has given them to Me, is greater than all; and no one is able to snatch them out of My Father's hand."

JOHN 11:25–27

25 Jesus said to her, "I am the resurrection and the life. He who believes in Me, though he may die, he shall live.

26 "And whoever lives and believes in Me shall never die. Do you believe this?"

27 She said to Him, "Yes, Lord, I believe that You are the Christ, the Son of God, who is to come into the world."

JOHN 12:24

24 "Most assuredly, I say to you, unless a grain of wheat falls into the ground and dies, it remains alone; but if it dies, it produces much grain."

JOHN 14:1–3,6,16–18,27–28

1 "Let not your heart be troubled; you believe in God, believe also in Me.

2 "In My Father's house are many mansions; if it were not so, I would have told you. I go to prepare a place for you.

3 "And if I go and prepare a place for you, I will come again and receive you to Myself; that where I am, there you may be also." . . .

6 Jesus said to him, "I am the way, the truth, and the life. No one comes to the Father except through Me. . . .

16 "And I will pray the Father, and He will give you another Helper, that He may abide with you forever—

17 "the Spirit of truth, whom the world cannot receive, because it neither sees Him nor knows Him; but you know Him, for He dwells with you and will be in you.

18 "I will not leave you orphans; I will come to you. . . .

27 "Peace I leave with you, My peace I give to you; not as the world gives do I give to you. Let not your heart be troubled, neither let it be afraid.

28 "You have heard Me say to you, 'I am going away and coming back to you.' If you loved Me, you would rejoice because I said, 'I am going to the Father,' for My Father is greater than I."

ROMANS 8:16,23,28,31–32,37–39

16 The Spirit Himself bears witness with our spirit that we are children of God. . . .

23 Not only that, but we also who have the firstfruits of the Spirit, even we ourselves groan within ourselves, eagerly waiting for the adoption, the redemption of our body. . . .

28 And we know that all things work together for good to those who love God, to those who are the called according to His purpose. . . .

31 What then shall we say to these things? If God is for us, who can be against us?

32 He who did not spare His own Son, but delivered Him up for us all, how shall He not with Him also freely give us all things? . . .

37 Yet in all these things we are more than conquerors through Him who loved us.

38 For I am persuaded that neither death nor life, nor angels nor principalities nor powers, nor things present nor things to come,

39 nor height nor depth, nor any other created thing, shall be able to separate us from the love of God which is in Christ Jesus our Lord.

ROMANS 14:7–9

7 For none of us lives to himself, and no one dies to himself.

8 For if we live, we live to the Lord; and if we die, we die to the Lord. Therefore, whether we live or die, we are the Lord's.

9 For to this end Christ died and rose and lived again, that He might be Lord of both the dead and the living.

ROMANS 15:4,13

4 For whatever things were written before were written for our learning, that we through the patience and comfort of the Scriptures might have hope. . . .

13 Now may the God of hope fill you with all joy and peace in believing, that you may abound in hope by the power of the Holy Spirit.

1 CORINTHIANS 13:9–13

9   For we know in part and we prophesy in part.

10 But when that which is perfect has come, then that which is in part will be done away.

11 When I was a child, I spoke as a child, I understood as a child, I thought as a child; but when I became a man, I put away childish things.

12 For now we see in a mirror, dimly, but then face to face. Now I know in part, but then I shall know just as I also am known.

13 And now abide faith, hope, love, these three; but the greatest of these is love.

1 CORINTHIANS 15:20–26,40–58 (New Living Translation)

20 But the fact is that Christ has been raised from the dead. He has become the first of a great harvest of those who will be raised to life again.

21 So you see, just as death came into the world through a man, Adam, now the resurrection from the dead has begun through another man, Christ.

22 Everyone dies because all of us are related to Adam, the first man. But all who are related to Christ, the other man, will be given new life.

23 But there is an order to this resurrection: Christ was raised first; then when Christ comes back, all his people will be raised.

24 After that the end will come, when he will turn the Kingdom over to God the Father, having put down all enemies of every kind.

25 For Christ must reign until he humbles all his enemies beneath his feet.

26 And the last enemy to be destroyed is death. . . .

40 There are bodies in the heavens, and there are bodies on earth. The glory of the heavenly bodies is different from the beauty of the earthly bodies.

41 The sun has one kind of glory, while the moon and stars each have another kind. And even the stars differ from each other in their beauty and brightness.

42 It is the same way for the resurrection of the dead. Our earthly bodies, which die and decay, will be different when they are resurrected, for they will never die.

43 Our bodies now disappoint us, but when they are raised, they will be full of glory. They are weak now, but when they are raised, they will be full of power.

44 They are natural human bodies now, but when they are raised, they will be spiritual bodies. For just as there are natural bodies, so also there are spiritual bodies.

45 The Scriptures tell us, "The first man, Adam, became a living person." But the last Adam—that is, Christ—is a life-giving Spirit.

46 What came first was the natural body, then the spiritual body comes later.

47 Adam, the first man, was made from the dust of the earth, while Christ, the second man, came from heaven.

48 Every human being has an earthly body just like Adam's, but our heavenly bodies will be just like Christ's.

49 Just as we are now like Adam, the man of the earth, so we will someday be like Christ, the man from heaven.

50 What I am saying, dear brothers and sisters, is that flesh and blood cannot inherit the Kingdom of God. These perishable bodies of ours are not able to live forever.

51 But let me tell you a wonderful secret God has revealed to us. Not all of us will die, but we will all be transformed.

52 It will happen in a moment, in the blinking of an eye, when the last trumpet is blown. For when the trumpet sounds, the Christians who have died will be raised with transformed bodies. And then we who are living will be transformed so that we will never die.

53 For our perishable earthly bodies must be transformed into heavenly bodies that will never die.

54 When this happens—when our perishable earthly bodies have been transformed into heavenly bodies that will never die—then at last the Scriptures will come true: "Death is swallowed up in victory.

55 O death, where is your victory? O death, where is your sting?"

56 For sin is the sting that results in death, and the law gives sin its power.

57 How we thank God, who gives us victory over sin and death through Jesus Christ our Lord!

58 So, my dear brothers and sisters, be strong and steady, always enthusiastic about the Lord's work, for you know that nothing you do for the Lord is ever useless.

2 CORINTHIANS 1:3–4

3   Blessed be the God and Father of our Lord Jesus Christ, the Father of mercies and God of all comfort,

4   who comforts us in all our tribulation, that we may be able to comfort those who are in any trouble, with the comfort with which we ourselves are comforted by God.

2 CORINTHIANS 5:1–8

1   For we know that if our earthly house, this tent, is destroyed, we have a building from God, a house not made with hands, eternal in the heavens.

2   For in this we groan, earnestly desiring to be clothed with our habitation which is from heaven,

3   if indeed, having been clothed, we shall not be found naked.

4   For we who are in this tent groan, being burdened, not because we want to be unclothed, but further clothed, that mortality may be swallowed up by life.

5   Now He who has prepared us for this very thing is God, who also has given us the Spirit as a guarantee.

6   So we are always confident, knowing that while we are at home in the body we are absent from the Lord.

7   For we walk by faith, not by sight.

8   We are confident, yes, well pleased rather to be absent from the body and to be present with the Lord.

PHILIPPIANS 1:20–23

20 according to my earnest expectation and hope that in nothing I shall be ashamed, but with all boldness, as always, so now also Christ will be magnified in my body, whether by life or by death.

21 For to me, to live is Christ, and to die is gain.

22 But if I live on in the flesh, this will mean fruit from my labor; yet what I shall choose I cannot tell.

23 For I am hard pressed between the two, having a desire to depart and be with Christ, which is far better.

PHILIPPIANS 3:20–21 (*New Living Translation*)

20 But we are citizens of heaven, where the Lord Jesus Christ lives. And we are eagerly waiting for him to return as our Savior.

21 He will take these weak mortal bodies of ours and change them into glorious bodies like his own, using the same mighty power that he will use to conquer everything, everywhere.

PHILIPPIANS 4:6–9

6   Be anxious for nothing, but in everything by prayer and supplication, with thanksgiving, let your requests be made known to God;

7   and the peace of God, which surpasses all understanding, will guard your hearts and minds through Christ Jesus.

8   Finally, brethren, whatever things are true, whatever things are noble, whatever things are just, whatever things are pure, whatever things are lovely, whatever things are of good report, if there is any virtue and if there is anything praiseworthy—meditate on these things.

9 The things which you learned and received and heard and saw in me, these do, and the God of peace will be with you.

1 THESSALONIANS 4:13–18

13 But I do not want you to be ignorant, brethren, concerning those who have fallen asleep, lest you sorrow as others who have no hope.

14 For if we believe that Jesus died and rose again, even so God will bring with Him those who sleep in Jesus.

15 For this we say to you by the word of the Lord, that we who are alive and remain until the coming of the Lord will by no means precede those who are asleep.

16 For the Lord Himself will descend from heaven with a shout, with the voice of an archangel, and with the trumpet of God. And the dead in Christ will rise first.

17 Then we who are alive and remain shall be caught up together with them in the clouds to meet the Lord in the air. And thus we shall always be with the Lord.

18 Therefore comfort one another with these words.

1 THESSALONIANS 5:8–10

8 But let us who are of the day be sober, putting on the breastplate of faith and love, and as a helmet the hope of salvation.

9 For God did not appoint us to wrath, but to obtain salvation through our Lord Jesus Christ,

10 who died for us, that whether we wake or sleep, we should live together with Him.

2 THESSALONIANS 2:16–17

16 Now may our Lord Jesus Christ Himself, and our God and Father, who has loved us and given us everlasting consolation and good hope by grace,

17 comfort your hearts and establish you in every good word and work.

2 TIMOTHY 1:12

12 For this reason I also suffer these things; nevertheless I am not ashamed, for I know whom I have believed and am persuaded that He is able to keep what I have committed to Him until that Day.

2 TIMOTHY 4:7–8

7 I have fought the good fight, I have finished the race, I have kept the faith.

8 Finally, there is laid up for me the crown of righteousness, which the Lord, the righteous Judge, will give to me on that Day, and not to me only but also to all who have loved His appearing.

TITUS 1:2

2 in hope of eternal life which God, who cannot lie, promised before time began.

TITUS 2:13

13 looking for the blessed hope and glorious appearing of our great God and Savior Jesus Christ.

HEBREWS 2:14–18

14 Inasmuch then as the children have partaken of flesh and blood, He Himself likewise shared in the same, that through death He might destroy him who had the power of death, that is, the devil,

15 and release those who through fear of death were all their lifetime subject to bondage.

16 For indeed He does not give aid to angels, but He does give aid to the seed of Abraham.

17 Therefore, in all things He had to be made like His brethren, that He might be a merciful and faithful High Priest in things pertaining to God, to make propitiation for the sins of the people.

18 For in that He Himself has suffered, being tempted, He is able to aid those who are tempted.

HEBREWS 4:14–16

14 Seeing then that we have a great High Priest who has passed through the heavens, Jesus the Son of God, let us hold fast our confession.

15 For we do not have a High Priest who cannot sympathize with our weaknesses, but was in all points tempted as we are, yet without sin.

16 Let us therefore come boldly to the throne of grace, that we may obtain mercy and find grace to help in time of need.

HEBREWS 11:13–16

13 These all died in faith, not having received the promises, but having seen them afar off were assured of them, embraced them and confessed that they were strangers and pilgrims on the earth.

14 For those who say such things declare plainly that they seek a homeland.

15 And truly if they had called to mind that country from which they had come out, they would have had opportunity to return.

16 But now they desire a better, that is, a heavenly country. Therefore God is not ashamed to be called their God, for He has prepared a city for them.

HEBREWS 13:5–6

5 Let your conduct be without covetousness; be content with such things as you have. For He Himself has said, "I will never leave you nor forsake you."

6 So we may boldly say: "The Lord is my helper; I will not fear. What can man do to me?"

1 PETER 5:6–7

6 Therefore humble yourselves under the mighty hand of God, that He may exalt you in due time,

7 casting all your care upon Him, for He cares for you.

1 JOHN 5:11,13

11 And this is the testimony: that God has given us eternal life, and this life is in His Son. . . .

13 These things I have written to you who believe in the name of the Son of God, that you may know that you have eternal life, and that you may continue to believe in the name of the Son of God.

REVELATION 1:17–18

17 And when I saw Him, I fell at His feet as dead. But He laid His right hand on me, saying to me, "Do not be afraid; I am the First and the Last.

18 "I am He who lives, and was dead, and behold, I am alive forevermore. Amen. And I have the keys of Hades and of Death."

REVELATION 14:13

13 Then I heard a voice from heaven saying to me, "Write: 'Blessed are the dead who die in the Lord from now on.'" "Yes," says the Spirit, "that they may rest from their labors, and their works follow them."

REVELATION 7:15–17

15 "Therefore they are before the throne of God, and serve Him day and night in His temple. And He who sits on the throne will dwell among them.

16 "They shall neither hunger anymore nor thirst anymore; the sun shall not strike them, nor any heat;

17 "for the Lamb who is in the midst of the throne will shepherd them and lead them to living fountains of waters. And God will wipe away every tear from their eyes."

REVELATION 21:1–7

1 Now I saw a new heaven and a new earth, for the first heaven and the first earth had passed away. Also there was no more sea.

2 Then I, John, saw the holy city, New Jerusalem, coming down out of heaven from God, prepared as a bride adorned for her husband.

3 And I heard a loud voice from heaven saying, "Behold, the tabernacle of God is with men, and He will dwell with them, and they shall be His people. God Himself will be with them and be their God.

4 And God will wipe away every tear from their eyes; there shall be no more death, nor sorrow, nor crying. There shall be no more pain, for the former things have passed away."

5 Then He who sat on the throne said, "Behold, I make all things new." And He said to me, "Write, for these words are true and faithful."

6 And He said to me, "It is done! I am the Alpha and the Omega, the Beginning and the End. I will give of the fountain of the water of life freely to him who thirsts.

7 "He who overcomes shall inherit all things, and I will be his God and he shall be My son."

REVELATION 21:22–26

22 But I saw no temple in it, for the Lord God Almighty and the Lamb are its temple.

23 The city had no need of the sun or of the moon to shine in it, for the glory of God illuminated it. The Lamb is its light.

24 And the nations of those who are saved shall walk in its light, and the kings of the earth bring their glory and honor into it.

25 Its gates shall not be shut at all by day (there shall be no night there).

26 And they shall bring the glory and the honor of the nations into it.

REVELATION 22:1–5

1 And he showed me a pure river of water of life, clear as crystal, proceeding from the throne of God and of the Lamb.

2   In the middle of its street, and on either side of the river, was the tree of life, which bore twelve fruits, each tree yielding its fruit every month. The leaves of the tree were for the healing of the nations.

3   And there shall be no more curse, but the throne of God and of the Lamb shall be in it, and His servants shall serve Him.

4   They shall see His face, and His name shall be on their foreheads.

5   There shall be no night there: They need no lamp nor light of the sun, for the Lord God gives them light. And they shall reign forever and ever.

You may want to select a few of these verses that minister to you most and make them your daily confession. Or you may desire to read through this entire chapter on a regular basis. Perhaps you know friends who would benefit from a positive word in this season of their life, and you can share the comfort of God's Word with them. Whatever our situation, the Word of God will sustain us. His Word is truth, and it will live and abide forever (Psalm 119:160; 1 Peter 1:23).

ABOUT THE AUTHOR

Gifted as a teacher, Tony Cooke has been serving the Body of Christ in various capacities since 1980. Currently, Tony teaches worldwide with an emphasis on strengthening churches and leaders. Tony's ministry travels have taken him to more than forty states and twenty countries. He enjoys helping believers reach their potential in Christ, helping leaders maximize their skills and effectiveness, and helping churches become healthy, vibrant, and strong.

For more than eighteen years, Tony served on staff at Kenneth Hagin Ministries—as Dean and instructor at Rhema Bible Training College, Senior Associate Pastor at Rhema Bible Church, Director of Rhema Ministerial Association International, and Director of Rhema Alumni Association.

A 1981 graduate of Rhema Bible Training College, Tony studied Religion at Butler University and received a Bachelor of Science degree in Church Ministries from North Central University.

Tony and his wife, Lisa, reside in Broken Arrow, Oklahoma, and are the parents of two adult children: Laura and Andrew.

If you would like to contact the author, you may do so at:

www.tonycooke.org